The Practice of Zen Meditation

愛宮眞備

THE PRACTICE OF ZEN MEDITATION

Hugo M. Enomiya-Lassalle

Compiled and edited by
Roland Ropers and Bogdan Snela

Translated from the German by
Michelle Bromley

The Aquarian Press
An Imprint of HarperCollins*Publishers*

The Aquarian Press
An Imprint of HarperCollins*Publishers*
77-85 Fulham Palace Road,
Hammersmith, London W6 8JB
1160 Battery Street
San Francisco, California 94111-1213

First published in German as *ZEN-Unterweisung* 1987
Published by Crucible 1990
This edition 1992
10 9 8 7 6 5 4 3 2 1

© Kösel-Verlag, Munich 1987
This English translation © The Aquarian Press 1990

A catalogue record for this book
is available from the British Library

ISBN 1 85538 313 6

Typeset by Harper Phototypesetters Limited, Northampton
Printed in Great Britain by The Bath Press, Bath, Avon

Contents

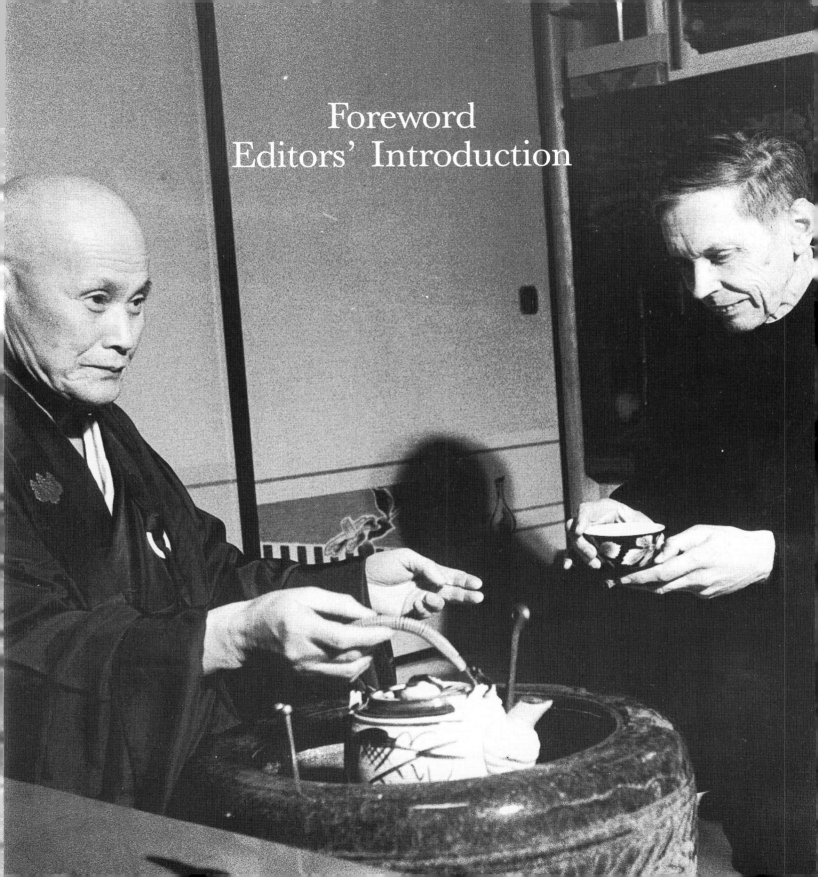

Foreword
Editors' Introduction

Foreword

The original texts for this book go back to a *sesshin* held in Japan in 1977 in my Zen Centre 'Shinmeikutsu'. One of the participants of this course recorded the daily lectures, the so-called *teishōs*, on tape and later transcribed these texts for publication. The editors of this volume, also Zen pupils of mine, have revised and updated these texts with my help and have provided this 'Zen Workbook' with clear illustrations and an informative appendix.

This book, *Zen Instruction*, is intended for all those who are interested in the practice of Zen meditation and/or would like to explore this study of a new consciousness. Although the comparison between Christian mysticism and Zen meditation is aptly and repeatedly made in these lectures (*teishōs*), this does not mean that the way of *Zazen* [sitting in Zen] described here is suitable only for Christians. In fact Buddhists as well as followers of other religions often take part in my Zen courses. Because Zen is not bound to any particular ideology, it can have a liberating effect for anyone and be useful in all situations of daily life. It will give me much pleasure, if this book proves to be of benefit to many people. Mature students of Zen as well as beginners should be informed about the arduous way to enlightenment in Zen meditation. May this book contribute to spreading a new consciousness for our troubled times.

Hugo M. Enomiya-Lassalle
Tokyo/Dietfurt a.d. Altmühl
1 December 1986

I am often asked by Christians, especially by Catholics, whether it is possible to practise Zen and still remain true to their Christian faith. To this question I usually reply that Zen is not a religion in the sense that Christianity is a religion. Therefore there is no reason why Zazen and Christianity should not coexist. The outer garment is of a different form and colour, but what is underneath, the heart, remains the same. And this heart, this experience is not embellished with any thoughts or philosophies. It is a pure fact, an experienced fact, in the same way that tasting tea is a fact. A cup of tea has no thoughts, no ideas, no philosophy. It tastes the same to Buddhists as it does to Christians. There is not the slightest difference there.

Koūn Yamada, born 1907, Zen master in Kamakura, Japan

Editors' Introduction

As the volume of Zen literature as grown over the last few years, it has also become increasingly confusing for the layman. Although a certain amount of knowledge can be gleaned from books, it is only through practical experience that real understanding is gained and nurtured. This is especially true for Zen: Zen meditation is not an acquired skill, but rather a way, *the* way leading inwards to the True Self.

Many people today suffer from the constraints placed on them by our exclusively rational way of thinking and they are beginning to look for a way out of this dilemma. There are countless 'meditation methods' available, all of which promise to lead out of this crisis. With such a large selection, however, it is often very difficult for people to make a choice, let alone evaluate the quality.

It is therefore advisable that each person should decide on just *one* way and not become further confused by trying many different methods. Among these methods Zen meditation can offer a wonderful opportunity for rediscovering the way back to the True Self. This way, however, can be very long and requires persistent practice and wholehearted effort to achieve the desired goal: Zen is not a quick method, but much rather a life's work.

People have to find a way back to themselves. This does not mean, however, that they should become increasingly I-orientated or egotistical. That would just make them even more deluded than they already are—a kind of 'narcissistic self-cultivation', a condition, unfortunately, strengthened by many of the 'meditation methods' presently offered. On the contrary, this sense of an individual self must be overcome in order to arrive at the deepest self, the essential nature. The Eastern methods of meditation, particularly Zen, offer an exceptional possibility for this. Being almost totally absorbed in the external world nowadays, we no longer know this inner self. It is the way to the inner life, to this deeper self, which should also reveal the True Nature of God, that Zen meditation points to.

Father Enomiya-Lassalle is both Zen master and Christian apostle, and with his immense experience he guides many followers safely and responsibly along the religious way.

Zen Instruction contains all the essential aspects of Zen meditation and also points beyond that to the successful integration of Christian and Eastern spirituality as realized by Enomiya-Lassalle. It should thus appeal to Christians and non-Christians alike.

A Jesuit, Hugo M. Enomiya-Lassalle has himself practised Zen meditation for nearly 50 years, and for over 20 years now has been running meditation courses in Japan and Europe. Thousands of people have taken part in these, including some who have themselves since become Zen masters and Zen teachers.

In this book Enomiya-Lassalle endeavours, as hardly anyone before has done, to integrate Eastern– and Western–Christian mysticism. Due to this remarkable synthesis he has become one of the most influential forerunners of this new integrated consciousness and here, for the first time, is published the complete seven-day instruction given during one of his Zen courses.

Because many Zen courses in Japan are run over a period of seven days, the lectures and instructions of Father Enomiya-Lassalle have also been arranged according to a seven-day programme. However, this is by no means intended to imply that enlightenment can be attained after just seven days.

In every Zen course the Zen master gives a so-called *teishō* once a day, which lasts 40 to 50 minutes. In this the most important aspects of Zen meditation are explained from different angles, in order to guide the trainees along the way to enlightenment. In contrast to many other Zen masters, whose teachings focus mainly on the solving of *kōans* (riddles), Enomiya-Lassalle also explains in great depth other aspects of Zen practice and meditation: sitting (*Zazen*), breathing, remaining silent, solving *kōans*, personal interviews with the master (*dokusan*), the stages of absorption and the relationship between Christian contemplation and Eastern enlightenment.

The present book is meant as an introduction and guide for the reader and trainee alike. The illustrations emphasize the practical nature of this work. Many of the photographs (though not all) are by Petra M. Kammann, who with great dedication also helped to produce this book in its present form. The appendix with practical exercises and information was conceived as an aid to beginners who do not have the opportunity to attend introductory courses or yoga classes, but who would like to enrol for a Zen-*sesshin*, which is intended only for experienced trainees.

In this context our thanks are also extended to Frau Susanne Hagenstein, Yoga teacher from Mühlheim a.M., to Frau Brita Dahlberg from the Frankfurt Ring and to Herr Andreas Heyden, T'ai Ch'i teacher from Frankfurt, who through their particular skills acted as models for correct posture and the exercises in the practical section.

The illustrations for breathing and for the stages of absorption, the information on the structure of Zen *sesshins* both in Europe and in Japan, and the addresses of centres suitable for Zen meditation and Christian contemplation are intended to serve as a reliable guide to those interested in deepening the practice of meditation. Thus this book is a standard work on Zen meditation—not just helpful to beginners, but fundamental for anyone concerned with the deeper experiences of Eastern and Western mysticism. It is recommended that this book be treated as a 'workbook' to use and to pass on, to consult, read and meditate upon. It is a book with which one works, be it as a Zen teacher, as a Zen student or as someone interested in Zen meditation and the new consciousness.

ROLAND ROPERS and BOGDAN SNELA
Düsseldorf/Munich, 11 November 1986
The 88th birthday of H.M. Enomiya-Lassalle

Editor's Note: H. M. Enomiya-Lassalle died on 7 July 1990.

Day one
Silence
Sitting
Breathing
Not-Thinking

Towards a New Rhythm of Life

We rise at 4 a.m. and not less than 20 minutes later the first formal period of meditation begins (see Appendix, Daily Programme in Japan, p. 113). Different *zendos* (meditation halls) may have different schedules depending on local conditions and customs. As an extreme example, for instance, during our first *sesshin* (days of spiritual collectedness) at Shinmeikutsu everyone had to get up at 3 a.m. and was expected to be sitting formally in their place 5 minutes later. This obviously precluded any chance for diversion. Here, however, we allow 20 minutes to give you the opportunity for a simple morning toilet. The men may forgo shaving if they want, as no one here will be offended. In fact Master Harada in Hosshinji used to forbid shaving, because it can lead to unnecessary distraction.

So do not concern yourselves with the unessential. The only important thing is to be on time. As we rise early in the morning it is advisable also to retire early at night. In fact it would be best if everyone retired and rose at the same times. Do not be surprised when you hear the sound of the gong in the

morning. Its purpose is to remind you to take your places within 5 minutes at the latest. The use of the gong to indicate the various times of the day is a long-standing tradition in Zen monasteries and one we carry on here too. During the *sesshin* everyone will be assigned a particular task, *samu*, to carry out. Whatever this may be, whether cleaning the rooms and corridors, helping in the kitchen or working in the garden, try and maintain a meditative awareness while doing it. The beginning and the end of this work period are both signalled by the striking of the gong. If you finish your particular job before the gong sounds, then help with another job until the end of that period is rung.

During a *sesshin* you should try to limit your food intake to about 70 per cent of your usual amount. There is no need for total fasting during extended periods of meditation; in fact the body is needed as a fundamental support in meditation.

People begin Zen training for a variety of reasons. Some may come to improve their physical or psychological well-being, others in the hope that Zen meditation will help in their religious life, to deepen their Christian faith and their life of prayer.

If you persist in the training with patient and wholehearted effort, favourable results will eventually arise. These effects will not necessarily be immediately obvious to you, as Zen training often works in a very subtle and profound way. There are people who achieve great insights on their very first *sesshin*, whereas others may sit for 10 years without gaining any insight. This, however, does not mean that they will not at some later time have an equally profound, or even deeper insight themselves. Just apply yourself

earnestly to Zen meditation and you will be enriched in any case.

In all the common rooms and at mealtimes try to remain inwardly concentrated. There is no need for the usual social niceties during a *sesshin*. Do not let your attention stray to your neighbour or beyond, but rather remain inwardly collected and alert. Concentrate continuously on your *kōan* (riddle) or on your breath, sinking deeper and deeper within yourself.

In this connection I am reminded of a story about a master of the tea ceremony and an American guest who came to visit him. After the master had prepared and served the tea, the American asked, 'Could you please explain all the details to me, how and why things are done in a certain way?' The master replied, 'Did you enjoy the tea?' 'Yes, it was delicious,' replied the American. 'That is all,' concluded the master. This story illustrates how we can become so preoccupied with details that we often miss the essential.

Deep within, in the Heart of man,
there God has chosen his resting place;
there he finds his joy—
If only we would do that too;
perceive those depths that lie within,
And leaving all behind
retire to rest therein
—Yet no one ever does.
And even so it may often be,
That a man upon his daily round
be urged ten times, or more, to look within
—Yet still no one ever does.

Johannes Tauler

Community of Silence

Whether in the house or outside, and especially at mealtimes, try not to gaze around unnecessarily, but rather keep inwardly focused. When the attention is turned inwards, silence arises naturally and this silence should always be both internal as well as external. If someone happens to forget this silence, do not respond to it, for the collectedness of the whole group will help them to find their way back to being silent more easily.

Most of the people attending a *sesshin* have probably never met one another before and first become acquainted in complete silence. This coming together in silence can be a most wonderful thing. It is extremely important to realize that with continued silent introspection, meditation becomes increasingly deeper, whereas that depth is quickly lost when one turns outwards. Although one is completely focused within oneself, a Zen *sesshin* is none the less very much a group effort. The more wholeheartedly all apply themselves, the more each supports the others and consequently the more the group comes together in a completely different way from what is normally experienced.

In Europe it is often said that silence is overemphasized at *sesshins*, but in Zen meditation this silence has a particular significance. It is not that there is anything fundamentally wrong with talking, but during long periods of meditation it can become an obstacle. We are not striving to become hermits here, who speak very little or not at all. But just for a while we must remain silent if we want to deepen our Zen practice. As many a Zen master has said, 'You need only open your mouth and you already succumb to 10,000 delusions.'

Spiritual Guidance: *Dokusan/Teishō*

The two most important things at a *sesshin* are meditation and spiritual guidance. Three times a day you will have the chance to come to *dokusan*, the personal interview with the master. In *dokusan* the master assesses the pupil's understanding and then gives him or her further pointers. After *dokusan* you should return straight to your place in the meditation hall. You can come to *dokusan* as often as you like. Sometimes, however, you may feel that it is pointless to come to *dokusan* because you have no more questions to ask or nothing particular has happened since the last time. You should come to me anyway and just say, 'Nothing has happened.' Just the act of going to *dokusan* itself is always enlivening and I want to help you progress a bit further. However, please do not ask theoretical questions during *dokusan*.

Upon entering the interview room and having made your bow, state what it is you are working on in the meditation. For example, 'I am counting the breath, I am working on this or that *kōan*, or I am practising "sitting in awareness".' Many people are not even conscious of what

they are doing and therefore do not know what to say. But for the master to give the appropriate guidance, he must know what you are practising. Only recount what you are experiencing during meditation and avoid raising personal problems or purely philosophical questions during *dokusan*.

Once a day I give *teishō*. Nowadays this Japanese word is usually translated as exposition. This *teishō* is neither a lecture nor a sermon in the conventional meaning, but something very typical and peculiar unto itself—a kind of preliminary instruction. Do not worry if you do not understand everything immediately. Zen masters usually comment on a *kōan* during *teishō* and at first this may be difficult to understand. Those who have been working on a *kōan* for some time will find it much easier to understand the Zen master during *teishō*. However, many practical things are also mentioned, which are particularly helpful to beginners in meditation, for *teishō* is not concerned with

theory, but with aspects that are beneficial to Zen training. But *teishō* is not as essential to a *sesshin* as the sitting and the guidance (*dokusan*).

As we slowly get deeper into meditation, we all have our own experiences and are always learning something new. When my first book on Zen, *Zen Way to Enlightenment*, was translated into Japanese many years ago, I asked the successor to the late Harada Rōshi, my first Zen master, to write an introduction for the Japanese edition. At the end of his introduction he wrote, 'When the author has attained enlightenment, he should write another book.' I can only agree with that, for it is only through constant practice that our experiences grow. None the less, we have to do, say, and write something for those who are just beginning to practise. First of all they must learn correct sitting (*Zazen*), which can be learned through a number of specific exercises often practised over a period of many months (see Appendix nos 1–28).

Posture

For *Zazen* we sit on a single round cushion, about 5–8 cm in height, which is placed either directly on the floor or on top of a ground mat (see Appendix no 21). While sitting, the right foot is placed on the left thigh and the left foot on the right thigh. The trunk should be kept vertical, as should the neck and head, which are just further extensions of the spinal column. In this way the tip of the nose and the navel will be in the same vertical line. To begin with, this posture is usually fairly difficult to maintain, but try to do it in such a way that no tension arises anywhere and the whole body remains relaxed.

This is the Lotus position, called *kekka* in Japanese (see Appendix no. 24) and is the suggested posture for *Zazen*. If this position is too difficult, you may modify it by placing only one foot on the opposite thigh and letting the other foot lie under the opposite thigh: the Half-Lotus position (see Appendix no. 25). This foot should be pulled in as close to the body as possible without actually sitting on it. An even easier variation is the Quarter-Lotus position: one foot lies on the

calf of the opposite leg, while the other foot lies under the opposite leg (see Appendix no. 26). Your eyes should be slightly open and focused on a point on the floor about one metre away or at the wall, if you meditate facing a wall.

Focusing your line of vision on a point should not be confused with concentrating on external objects, for your real concentration must be directed inwards. The eyes are only kept open to help prevent distracting mental images from arising. Those who strive for beautiful pictures and experiences should

> *When man sits,*
> *then the coarse passions subside*
> *and the luminous mind*
> *arises in awareness:*
> *Thus consciousness is illuminated.*
>
> Meister Eckhart

close their eyes, but this can then no longer be called Zen meditation. In Zen all distractions must be firmly restrained. The master quickly recognizes your distractedness and tiredness and will either shout or deal you a blow. Do not be alarmed by this, for its purpose is not to foster total obedience, but to encourage you to remain alert and to loosen up tense muscles. For this reason the blows are aimed at central acupuncture points, and are a means to urge you to remain on the right path.

Many of you will find it very difficult to meditate without a subject, without any kind of mental image, but the master will guide and direct you so that you may progress deeper into meditation.

Breathing as a Way to Not-Thinking

One of the most important requirements for penetrating into meditation is correct breathing. You should breathe through the nose, and deeply, from the diaphragm (see Appendix nos 40 and 41). The breath itself should be deep and calm. Do not pause for any length of time between the inhalation and the exhalation and never hold the breath.

Allow the breath to flow naturally. This deep breathing from the diaphragm will aid circulation and have a calming effect on the nervous system. Mental and emotional composure are essential for meditation; once the body is calm they will arise more easily.

I advise you to concentrate first on your breathing; this will enable you to clear away thoughts, notions and pictures more readily during meditation. Either count each breath or just concentrate on it without counting. Count only from 1 to 10 and then start again. The inhalations are counted on the odd numbers 1, 3, 5, 7, 9 and the exhalations on the even numbers 2, 4, 6, 8, 10. If you are distracted you can just count the inhalations and to counteract drowsiness count just the exhalations (see Appendix nos 42–5). When concentrating on the breath without counting, mentally follow the breath—when breathing in, pay attention only to the inhalation and when breathing out, pay attention only to the exhalation.

Concentrating on the breath is a very ancient practice, which supposedly goes back to the time of the Buddha or even earlier. Its purpose is gradually to eliminate everything else, so that inner calm can arise. It is surprisingly effective and very good to start with.

One should not practise counting the breath half-heartedly; nothing should be of greater importance than the counting itself—from 1 to 10. As one penetrates deeper and deeper into meditation through counting the breath, it is possible to achieve enlightenment through this exercise alone.

For those new to Zen meditation it is advisable at first just to concentrate on the breathing. Later we will learn of other possibilities that take us deeper into meditation.

Difficulties with Not–Thinking

Physical posture is essential in getting the body ready for meditation. When the breath flows correctly and the spine is kept upright, then the blood can circulate freely. *Zazen* is generally considered of benefit to physical health, and people who practise Zen often live well into old age. Most important, however, is the inner attitude, and correct posture and breathing serve this purpose. The difficulty lies in letting go of all thoughts. Master Dōgen (AD 1200–53), the founder of the Japanese Sōtō School, expressed it as follows: 'Think of not-thinking.'

In Japan there are two different Zen schools, *Sōtō* and *Rinzai*. In the Sōtō School one practises without a purpose or aim and sits facing the wall. In the Rinzai School one works with a *kōan* and sits facing the room. Here we practise *Zazen* facing the wall as in the Sōtō tradition, but also work with a *kōan* as in the Rinzai School.

To start with, thinking without an object will be difficult for you, but with continued practice you will begin to understand what is meant. Try not to doze off or fall asleep. When you arrive at that inner attitude where active thinking ceases, you will gradually penetrate into the depths of stillness. Normally we would consider rational thought as the height of a person's abilities. However, once having reached this state of profound stillness, even if only for a brief moment, all the theoretical problems about not-thinking will disappear. Have faith in the guidance of the Zen master, for he has practical human understanding and knows how to deal with the problems of daily life.

Not everything of a spiritual nature can be measured. Even people who have a positive attitude to meditation, especially some scientists, still insist on trying to measure this activity, which is not measurable. We must always differentiate between what is referred to as the psyche and the actual spirit.

The traditional aim of Zen and Yoga has always been a spiritual one. That is the basis of their link with Christianity and from that level alone can the highest experiences be understood. In Yoga, for instance, there are many preparatory exercises, which can be an aid to spiritual development. In the final stage, however, complete stillness is the most important thing.

Day 2
The *Kōan*
'Just Sitting'
The Master
Sitting in a Group

Working with *Kōans*

Having spoken about outer and inner posture and attitude yesterday, let us take a closer look today at the way the group works together during a Zen *sesshin* and the relationship between the master and the pupils.

Westerners seem to have particular difficulty in learning to let go of reason, will and memory, in order to find a way to absolute stillness. A traditional method of the Zen School for overcoming this problem has been to practise with a *kōan*. It is a fact that most Zen pupils are able to attain enlightenment with the help of this. The *kōan* is a problem which cannot be solved through logical thinking; an unsolvable riddle, unsolvable because it contains a contradication. Most *kōans* are the recorded sayings of famous Zen masters, uttered in specific situations. Let us take an example: a monk asked Master Chao-chou (Jap. Joshu), who lived in China from AD 778 to 897, whether a dog has Buddha-nature or not. Chao-chou said, 'Wu' (Jap. 'Mu', i.e. nothing). With that reply the master neither said 'yes' nor 'no'. The monk knew the Buddha taught that all sentient beings have Buddha-nature, yet hesitated as to whether even a dog could be a Buddha. Therefore the master did not answer, 'Yes, of course even a dog has Buddha-nature!' He tried to prevent the monk from attempting to understand Buddhism rationally. He wanted him to strive for a higher comprehension of reality, where all contradictions are resolved of their own accord.

At another time a monk asked the same master, 'Master, I am still a beginner, show me the way.' Chao-chou said, 'Have you had your breakfast yet?' The monk replied, 'Yes, I have had breakfast.' Then Chao-chou said, 'Go and wash your eating bowls.'

Yet another monk asked the master, 'What is the meaning of the First Patriarch's (Bodhidharma, who came to China from India) coming from the West?' Answer: 'The oak tree in front of the garden.' Hakuin (1685–1768 in Japan) clapped his hands; then he silently raised one hand and asked, 'What is the sound of one hand?'

No-I

There are two kinds of No-I. For example, take a person who is weak in body and mind. He is frightened of everyone, he destroys his life energy and is influenced by all outer circumstances. He does not get angry, even when insulted; nor does it bother him if he is rejected, but he just drags himself off mutely to somewhere else. His knowledge does not increase and he believes that the No-I he has reached is sufficient.

Such a person is a torn rice-sack, bloated because he has stuffed himself with himself at the swine trough, an ignorant fool. He does not embody the true No-I . . .

If you want to be in harmony with the true, pure No-I, you must be prepared to let go of your hold when hanging from a sheer precipice, to die and to return to life. Only then can you attain the true I of the four virtues of Nirvana.

Zen master Hakuin (1685–1768)

When one hears these dialogues between master and pupil, one becomes confused and asks oneself, 'What has the answer actually got to do with the question?'

There is in fact no direct connection between question and answer. If a connection were to exist in spite of this, then the *kōan* would no longer be a *kōan*, for the purpose of the *kōan* is to lead the pupil into an inescapable impasse. How is it that such a *kōan* can lead to the emptying of consciousness and further still to enlightenment itself? First the pupil will try to find a logical solution, but whatever he presents to the master will be rejected, unless it arises from the realm of intuitive thought. It will therefore also be of little use to him to present an answer which he has heard from someone else who has already attained enlightenment. For the master will immediately ask further questions to determine whether the pupil has really 'understood'. After this fruitless effort the pupil will finally give up the attempt to find a logical solution. Only then does the correct work with the *kōan* begin. He now no longer actually thinks about the *kōan*, but he has it on his mind constantly, day and night. An intense inner dilemma then arises, in which he can neither find an answer nor any longer drop the *kōan*. If he now continues working on the *kōan* with great intensity, he will arrive at a point where he becomes one with the *kōan*. He will become the *kōan*, the 'nothing' or the 'hand'. In this situation the entire consciousness has become filled with the *kōan*. Still he perseveres and continues to practise until the *kōan* suddenly disappears from his consciousness. At this instant the consciousness has become completely emptied and not even *satori*, enlightenment, the aspired goal can penetrate it. Now he is very near to enlightenment.

He must, however, continue practising with the utmost effort—without any reflection—and without directing his attention to any specific object. The consciousness must remain 'totally empty', otherwise the opportunity passes by. If he succeeds, then only a small spur will be necessary to open up the spirit to the new seeing, in which enlightenment takes place. Thus *satori* is generally precipitated by a sense perception, a sound that pierces the ear or an object that catches the eye, maybe even an emotion. This presupposes that such realization occurs completely unexpectedly and independent of meditation. Control on the part of the subject is not possible. This description may be too simplified and schematic, but it is only meant to indicate how working on a *kōan* can lead to enlightenment.

As I have already mentioned, the *kōan* is not used by all schools in the same way. In the Rinzai School, where *kōans* are systematically worked through, no one *kōan* is used exclusively throughout the training. One works with a succession of *kōans* in a particular order, whereby the spirit is gradually prepared for the final enlightenment. This is sometimes referred to as '*kōan* Zen' and is a transformation of thought patterns along strictly Buddhist lines; it is therefore less suitable and also less effective for Christians than for Buddhists. This does not, however, imply that a Christian must become a Buddhist in order to attain enlightenment.

There are a total of some 1,700 *kōans*. These can be found and read in various collections, such as the *Mumonkan* and the

Hekiganroku. The *Mumonkan* is a collection of 48 *kōans* by Zen Master Mumon and was originally published in China towards the end of the Southern Sung-Dynasty (thirteenth century AD). The commentary to each *koan* by Master Mumon, who compiled them, is extremely direct and points to the essential aspects. In Zen circles one usually begins with the *Mumonkan*, especially since the 48 *kōans* are outstanding and Mumon's commentaries are extremely lively. Using the *kōan* 'Mu' as an example, let us then return to the *koan* for a careful consideration of its use.

The kōan 'Mu'

A monk once asked Master Joshu, 'Has a dog Buddha-nature or not?' Joshu said, 'Mu!'

Mumon's Commentary: In the study of Zen, the barriers set up by the old masters have to be broken through. If one desires incomparable *satori*, then one has to eradicate the discriminating mind completely. Those who do not pass through the barrier and eradicate the discriminating mind are nothing but ghostly spectres haunting about in grasses and trees. Now tell me: What is this barrier of the Zen masters? Just this 'Mu'—that is the barrier of Zen and for this reason it is called the 'gateless barrier of Zen'.

Those who have overcome the barrier will not only see Joshu clearly, but will walk hand in hand with all the masters of the past and see them face to face. You will see with the same eye with which they see and hear with the same ear. Would that not be wonderful? Do you not want to overcome the barrier? Then concentrate on this 'Mu' with your 360 bones and 84,000 pores and transform your whole body into one big search. Work diligently on it day and night. Do not attempt any nihilistic or dualistic interpretations. It is as if you had gulped down a red-hot iron ball and cannot now spit it out. Completely discard your illusory, discriminating knowledge and your hitherto accumulated learning and work still harder. After a while your efforts will bear fruit, all distinctions (for example inside and outside) will become naturally one. You will be bewildered—like someone who has had a wonderful dream: one only knows it in oneself. Suddenly you break through the barrier. You will startle heaven and shake the earth.

It is as though you had seized General Kan's big sword. If you meet the Buddha, you kill him. If you encounter the old masters, you kill them. You will become completely free on the edge of life and death, and you will live a life of great joy and total freedom in the six realms and the four modes of life.

How shall one strive for it? With all your might, work on this 'Mu' and become 'Mu'. If you do not stop in your striving and do not waver, then you will see how the darkness brightens immediately once the Dharma candle is lit.

Shikantaza—Concentrated Awareness

So far I have explained the methods of following the breath and of working on a *kōan* as a means for reaching a state of absorption. In *shikantaza*, sitting in awareness, one's entire attention is directed solely to sitting. One just sits there and allows whatever arises to arise. One does not watch oneself, but remains completely passive. It is a very difficult way to follow, because one has to walk it without any aids. The way to enlightenment through *shikantaza* usually takes longer than the training with a *kōan*. With *shikantaza* your collectedness must have very strong roots and be as solid as a mountain, just like Mount Fuji. *Shikantaza* is a state of heightened and concentrated awareness in which one is neither exalted nor impetuous and naturally never inattentive.

Master Harada describes *shikantaza* in the following way: 'It is like Mount Fuji majestically towering over the East China Sea. But this comparison is still far too weak. Actually one should say: *Zazen* is a feeling, so solid, that it is as if the cushion had become the world and the whole universe was filling the abdomen. The green mountains stand immovable. The white clouds come and go.'

Make use of this image. When you sit, become Mount Fuji. Just let your thoughts come and go and remain unmoved, as if they were passing clouds. Whether the sky is clear or overcast, the mountain stays the same.

The clouds—your thoughts—pass by. The mountain always maintains its original form and this original form is the most profound and true nature. If you keep this in mind, then it will not seem difficult to let go of logical thoughts. In no circumstances, however, allow yourself to doze off, for that is dead Zen and is far worse than having many thoughts.

In Buddhist terms, the purpose of Zen training is to become aware of 'Buddha-nature'. This does not mean, however, that it is a practice only for Buddhists. On the contrary, it refers to a more universal concept, that of the 'dual nature' of man. One aspect being that part of our existence which we all are conscious of. But that is not all, for man also partakes of an indivisible and absolute existence which is the basis of all things. According to Buddhist teaching, man should not only have a share in this absolute existence, but must become aware of this state. The moment this happens, man discovers that what he previously held to be his Self is in fact not really, not in the fullest sense, his True Self. Thus awareness arises of the other side of his nature, of the transcendent, absolute aspect. The term 'enlightenment' tries to render perceptible the experience of this awareness.

This experience must be further deepened by regular and persistent Zen practice, gradually approaching what St Paul expressed as, 'I live, yet not I, but Christ liveth in me.' (Galatians 2:20).

Guidance through a Zen Master

In Zen the guidance of the Zen master is of prime importance. In the East the relationship between master and pupil has always been closer than in the West. This becomes particularly evident in Zen, for the most profound experience, *Satori* (enlightenment), is not passed on through words or writing, but through *ishin-denshin*: from soul to soul or from heart to heart.

It was in this way that Kaysapa became the Buddha's first successor. He inherited the task of continuing the founder's work through a spiritual succession rather than as an assignee. Kaysapa did the same before his death, as did all of his successors and for this reason they are called the Patriarchs in Zen Buddhism. This way it developed in response to the subtle nature of the transmission, for what was handed down, and is still being handed down today, is not a teaching or philosophy that can be acquired by study, but is a distinct and unique experience. Although there is a teaching and philosophy in Buddhism that can be studied, here we are concerned with something completely different—a spiritual experience or intuition which cannot be expressed in words, but is recognized with certainty by the master when the pupil attains it. Zen has always valued the transmission more highly than Buddhist teaching or philosophy, which may change in the course of time. The importance of this guidance or transmission from soul to soul through the Zen master does not apply only

scripture. In this way it can be assured that the essence of the experience will not be falsified. Of course the assistance of a spiritual guide has been emphasized in Christianity, especially when one penetrates into the deeper regions of the life of prayer, where the devotee cultivates a more inward-directed attitude than when he or she just remains on the surface and is subject to many external distractions.

In Zen this guidance is important right from the beginning, because one is attempting to penetrate into the unconscious immediately. For this purpose I-orientated thought-processes are brought to a halt and one keeps completely still within. Just because of this lack of I-activity, when one does not do anything oneself, something happens or can happen. As long as one still has no experience in this field, it is particularly necessary to have guidance, so that one does not go astray.

Even after a particularly clear insight, the guidance of a Zen master is still of immeasurable value. With good guidance one advances more quickly and has a greater chance of attaining enlightenment. However progress in *Zazen* and the attainment of *satori* do not depend solely on the guidance of the Zen master, but also on other things—one's own temperament and the amount of effort one puts into the practice. As to these the Zen master can neither add to nor take away anything.

As a rule, during the several days of our *sesshin*, you will come to see the Zen master two or three times a day. Generally these visits are very short, the pupil staying in the interview room—*dokusanshitsu*—with the master for only a few minutes or even less.

in the case where the continuation of the tradition concerns eminent figures of Zen Buddhism, but also applies to each individual case where a pupil seeks to follow the guidance of a Zen master. Even today the axiom is still valid: *ishin-denshin*, direct transmission by the heart and not by word or

Often only a short question is asked and an even shorter answer is given. And yet this time is sufficient for the master to determine the spiritual state of the pupil and to give the guidance appropriate at the moment. Often

Buddha, Confucius and Lao Tzu in front of the vinegar cask. Each one dips his finger into the vinegar to taste it. Buddha finds it bitter, Confucius sour and Lao Tzu finds it sweet. All is a question of consciousness.

it is just a brief incentive which the pupil does not really understand at the time, and which only becomes clear to him when he returns to his cushion in the Zen hall.

One should look for a Zen master whom one can trust completely; if one can be found who, though a Buddhist, is also open and sympathetic to Christianity, then that would be ideal. Once having found a master, one should stick with him. However, one should not forget the 'inner master' whom one can also follow. When you have genuinely gained a high degree of freedom from all things, then you will hear the voice of this 'inner master'.

For those who have only worked on themselves a little, the clear receptivity necessary for hearing this voice will be lacking. They may too easily mistake the 'inner master' for themselves.

The Zen way, with or without guidance, is not a leisurely stroll, nor is it something that quickly transpires or passes over, but is a life's work. We have to clear away many hindrances in order to become completely 'empty'. Because we did not come into this world 'empty' and in the course of our life so far have accumulated many impressions, it is extremely difficult to let go of everything completely.

To Confucius, this realization became the guide for his whole life: 'At fifteen I set my heart on learning, at thirty I stood firm, at forty I was free from doubts, at fifty I understood the will of heaven, at sixty I was still striving to understand further, at seventy I could follow the desires of my heart without transgressing what is right.'

Sitting as a Group

When Zen meditation is practised in a group, it is necessary to observe certain rules. These may at first appear strange to the Westerner and some may wonder whether each detail is absolutely necessary. The answer to that is: Zen in its present form has a tradition of hundreds of years. During that time, certain rules and practices have become established which we, in turn, should simply accept, especially as they are not contrary to common sense and certainly have a justifiable reason.

The hall in which *Zazen* is practised is called a *dōjō*. The floor of the *dōjō* is laid out with mats. In traditional monasteries, however, the monks sit on wooden platforms on cushions (*zafu*) which lie on flat ground mats or blankets (*zaniku*), of approximately one square metre in size. At the entrance to the Zen hall the shoes are taken off and placed exactly parallel, with the toes facing outwards, away from the *dōjō*. One enters the room slowly, with the left foot first, but leaves with the right foot first.

Before taking your place on the cushion, and while facing the wall, you should raise your hands in a humble gesture, in *gasshō*; for this the palms of the hands are placed together and one bows as a gesture of greeting. This is an expression of your inner collectedness and harmony with the whole.

As far as possible never walk across the *dōjō*, but rather keep to the sides of the room near the walls in a clockwise direction. Everyone should be inwardly concentrated and keep the eyes lowered.

After everyone has settled in a comfortable sitting position by gently rocking the upper part of the body back and forth, a bell is rung three times to begin the *Zazen* period.

The Zen master oversees the participants and will correct a person's posture when necessary. To help with this, he carries a long wooden stick, which is flat at one end, the *kyosaku*—warning staff. With it he occasionally strikes one or two blows to the muscles on either side of the neck. This is not meant as some sort of punishment or humiliation, but rather as a spur and release from tension. The areas struck contain certain important acupuncture points and are also the meeting point of approximately 50 nerve endings.

The word *kyosaku* is formed from the words: *kyo* = attention and *saku* = staff. The blow from the *kyosaku* rouses the attention and helps to restore concentration and dispel any tiredness, distraction or agitation. When using the *kyosaku*, it is important that both the

person dealing the blows as well as the one receiving them harmonize their gestures. Both should breathe out at the same time as the blows are struck; since one naturally turns the head away from the shoulder being struck, the corresponding neck-muscles are stretched, making the blow more effective. First the Zen master or his assistant gently touches the shoulder of the meditator, who then bows in *gasshō* and lowers the head, first to the left and then to the right in order to expose the respective shoulder. After receiving the blows the trainee again bows.

The use of the *kyosaku* may also be requested by bowing and raising folded hands. This request should only be made if there is a genuine need for it. The mutual understanding between the two people involved in the use of the *kyosaku* should be thought of as follows: The trainee, 'Please, help me to become inwardly collected.' The master, 'I will gladly help you.' After the blows: the trainee, 'I thank you for your assistance.' The master, 'I thank you for allowing me to be of assistance.'

Everything is your life

Whatever you encounter, day and night, is your life; you should therefore give yourself to each situation as it arises from moment to moment. Use your life energy towards that purpose, so that from the circumstances that befall you, you may create a harmonious life with all things in their rightful place.

Zen master Dōgen (AD 1200–53)

One should not leave the room during *Zazen* but if it is essential, one should first bow to the wall and then to the Zen master before leaving one's place and the Zen hall noiselessly. One may not re-enter before the next break. The end of the meditation period is also announced by the bell. On leaving the room one bows in the same way as when one entered.

To help relax the limbs, especially knees and feet (see Appendix nos 29–35), it is customary to interrupt the *Zazen* periodically with ten minutes of *kin-hin*, a walking exercise. During this exercise one always walks in a clockwise direction. To practise *kin-hin* well is considered very difficult (see Appendix nos 36–9). During its practice, the left hand is made into a fist with the thumb against the palm and the latter pointing downward; this fist is then placed just above the stomach on the solar plexus, so that the base of the thumb touches the body. The right hand is then placed over it, enclosing the back of the left hand, with the forearms kept horizontal. The gaze is directed towards the floor, about three metres ahead. The eyes should not wander about.

To start, the right foot moves half a step forward. On lowering the foot, the outer edge is put down first and then the weight is shifted to the front of the big toe. As the rest of the foot is lowered, it becomes almost anchored to the ground. The attention is focused on the big toe and the left thumb.

As the foot is put down, the leg straightens and the weight is shifted onto it; this straightens the knee and then the back. The chin is always pushed slightly in and the shoulders hang naturally. It should feel as though one were pushing up through the ceiling with the top of the head.

Meditation continues during *kin-hin* as in *Zazen*. A Zen master once said that *kin-hin* should be like the gait of an elephant or of a duck, slow and deliberate, the centre of gravity remaining in the abdomen (*hara*).

The beginning and end of *kin-hin* are marked by the clapping of two wooden clappers. When *kin-hin* finishes, everyone returns to his or her place quickly and in single file. Before sitting down everyone bows in *gasshō*, first to the room and then to the wall. Both these bows express gratitude to all the participants for having the opportunity of practising together. *Gasshō* is always an expression of this inner bond of brotherhood.

Day three
Temptation
Seeing Into One's True Nature
Little Enlightenment

Makyō: Eruptions of Psyche into Spirit

Today we are going to take a closer look at the process that begins to unfold as Zen meditation deepens. *Makyō* means, more or less, 'the world of demons'. This refers to such apparitions as arise visually and sometimes audibly, but cannot be classified as hallucinations, because they are not due to illness, nervousness or natural inclination. But they occur quite naturally to anyone training persistently, and are in fact a consequence of intense concentration. According to Zen masters, these phenomena are pictures or voices which surface from the unconscious, when ordinary consciousness is vigorously suppressed as in Zen meditation. These contents are always naturally present, but because the attention is fully occupied with conscious activity, they do not normally rise to the surface. These *makyō*–manifestations are seen with half-open eyes and are therefore not inner visions, but rather give the impression of being external phenomena. At their extreme they are very strong; one can see imagined figures appear before the eyes, as if they were really there.

These manifestations may be pleasant or unpleasant. To a Buddhist, for example, a representation of Kannon, goddess (sometimes god) of compassion, may appear, whom untold generations of Buddhists have revered and who is therefore imprinted in their memory; or a Christian may see images of Jesus, Mary or of angels. But these images can also be terrifying, as for example when they appear in the threatening form of demons or wild animals. It follows from the diversity of these manifestations that the 'vision' is not the result of a strong desire for

it. On the contrary, it arises as a result of the effort to cut off all desire and thoughts during *Zazen*. *Makyō* does not necessarily appear as people, animals or other figures. In fact it more commonly takes the form of a different type of vision, in phenomena of light and dark. For example clouds or shadows may appear before the eyes and seem to move and grow stronger or weaker. Some people experience this before an operation, when going under an anaesthetic. In fact the first

time I experienced *makyō* I was vividly reminded of the anaesthesia when operated on to remove a bullet in a field hospital during the First World War.

There are many kinds of light phenomena. For instance it may feel as though one's focus is shifting and then a point within it may burst into many sparks, like fireworks exploding and dispersing into many colours in all directions; or it may seem as if one is looking through a kaleidoscope. Sometimes one sees planes of violet light of various sizes. More often, though, white or yellow light appears and can be so strong that it gives the impression of the whole Zen hall being on fire, except that the light seems cool, rather like a fire on a black and white film. Sometimes it is like summer lightning. During night sittings in the open air, silverlight– *makyō*—as it could be called—occasionally occurs. This is of great beauty and makes the whole field of vision down to the last blade of grass appear silvered. At times other phenomena also occur such as a vigorous jolt in the body, followed by brightness, and the impression of the whole body being lifted up.

Manifestations of darkness can take the form of a seemingly impenetrable black wall and one literally feels as though one were facing the 'void'. When encountering *makyō*, the basic rule is to ignore it, regardless of whether it is pleasant or unpleasant. Even if the Buddha himself should appear, he is to be ignored. The Zen masters are in complete accord about it. If in spite of this one nevertheless pursues *makyō*, a lot of time may be lost, for as long as one remains consciously involved in it, real progress ceases and enlightenment remains impossible. On the other hand, the occurrence of *makyō* is seen as a sign that one is doing *Zazen* correctly and to that extent it is desirable, but for no other reason. Generally these phenomena disappear as soon as one stops the *Zazen*, but a particularly strong *makyō* may persist despite one's efforts to get rid of it. Do not conclude from this, however, that the more often *makyō* occurs, the more progress is being made. In fact at a later stage progress is marked by its non–occurrence.

A pupil once came to his Zen master and said that during meditation the strong conviction arose in him that he should stop. This is the worst kind of *makyō*! Do not yield to anything, do not let anything approach!

The same is expressed in the Jesus-prayer of the Hesychasts where one is enjoined not to give in even should Christ or the Mother of God, or angels appear.

Zen leads man into the realm of the pure spirit. The pure spirit, which knows neither psyche nor body, is God. The long journey of Zen meditation leads to that place. The true Christian mystics have always strictly advised against paying attention to any psychic phenomena, inner voices or similar experiences. The Zen masters, too, agree that one becomes separated from the pure spirit if one yields to these visions and related phenomena.

Saint Augustine says:
Do not search outside;
look within yourself,
truth lies in the inner man.

Meister Eckhart

Approaching One's True Nature

Those who are to some extent familiar with Christian mysticism will find many similarities when studying Zen. The converse also holds for Japanese, well-versed in Zen, reading the writings of Christian mystics, even though this literature is not particularly well known. After the First World War the previous long period of intolerance towards

case in man's cultural history, to a counter movement in its favour. This movement, however, lacked the strength and momentum to survive the political upheavals, both foreign and internal, that followed. Yet it was just this very fear of the times that together with, among other things, the rejection of rationalism in the religious sphere, awakened a longing for religious experience and mysticism.

The official Christian attitude to these

aspirations was still, however, mostly one of disapproval, and so many people, Christians included, turned to the non-Christian Eastern religions, which seemed to offer more scope for developing this mystical side of the religious life. In this roundabout way many people have learned about Christian mysticism, while others joined the Eastern religions. All of this seems to be gradually leading to a completely new and highly desirable discovery of mysticism. It is therefore quite relevant to discuss the connections between Christian mysticism and the Zen experience. From our previous discussion of Zen meditation and enlightenment, it must certainly have become clear that Zen meditation points *directly* to the *Absolute*, without any detours. The question is whether there is also a Christian meditation, which like *Zazen* directly aims at the Absolute? In Christian terms that would mean: a direct experience of God. Certainly every form of Christian medication strives for the Absolute, for God. Meditation should lead to a clearer understanding of God and a more perfect

> *Time and space are fragments,*
> *but God is one.*
> *Should man then recognize God,*
> *he must recognize him*
> *beyond time and space;*
> *for God is neither this nor that*
> *like these earthly multifarious things;*
> *for God is one.*
>
> Meister Eckhart

love of God, which inherently includes the love of one's fellow men. That is the aim of all Christian asceticism. The question remains, though, whether there is only the one kind of Christian meditation in which the aim is the contemplation of God, as is the usual custom, or whether there is also a meditation which leads to a more intuitive and direct realization of God.

According to the view of most theologians it is impossible for man to attain a complete intuitive realization of God in this life. The *visio beatifica*, the blissful contemplation of God, can only occur after death. 'For there shall no man see me [God], and live.' (Exodus 33:20), or as St John saw it, 'No man hath seen God at any time; the only begotten Son, which is in the bosom of the Father, he hath declared him.' (John 1:18). Nevertheless, both the Church Fathers and the mystics speak of a beholding of God, which is also called an experiential realization of God in contrast to a realization of God based on faith. In the same way Zen describes seeing into one's own True Nature or *satori* as a direct experience and not as a theoretical understanding.

Rather than seeking proof of God's existence, people today desire an experience of God. This divine experience, though, should not be thought of as experiencing God in the sense of a person, in other words as a concept, as is the case for those who have already found God. What is experienced is the ground from which all things spring, the very mystery our longing draws us towards, that which supports our life and on which everything rests; that which moves us deeply; which illuminates all the senses and all beauty. This is often described as an existential experience, which it truly is. In studying the writings of the mystics, we will find that Christian mysticism is a way towards divine experience and beyond that to a divine *union with God* and the entire way will be seen to have many similarities with Zen.

Seeing into the Nature of God according to Ruysbroeck

It is a long way to great *satori*, deep enlightenment. The following passage from the Dutch mystic Jan van Ruysbroeck (1294–1381) is very helpful to an understanding of Zen and in particular of enlightenment:

> You must know, that the intrinsic nature of the spirit directly and constantly receives Christ at the level of Pure Nature. For the existence and the life, which we are in God, in our eternal image, and which we have in our intrinsic nature, that is without mediation and without separation (eternally united with God). . .and therefore the spirit intrinsically possesses God at the level of Pure Nature, and God possesses the spirit; for it lives in God and God lives in it, and in its uppermost regions the spirit is capable of directly receiving God's clarity and everything that it can effect. . .But it does not follow from this that everyone is a saint from birth: This immanent nature is of itself neither holy nor blessed, for all people, good and bad alike, have it. However, it is certainly this, which is the cause of holiness and bliss.

For the understanding of this passage one should bear in mind, that the 'Pure Nature' Ruysbroeck speaks of refers to the intrinsic nature of man, regardless of whether it is elevated through grace or not, in other words, it includes all non-Christians as well. This parallels Zen thought, which always considers nature in this way. Here, for instance, it would mean that everyone by nature has the innate potential to attain enlightenment. In Buddhism, however, this is not related to Christ, but rather it is said, that all beings have Buddha-nature.

When considering the mystical experience itself, Ruysbroeck says, among other things:

Through the touching of the soul, through the birth of the Son, through eternal wisdom a brilliant light is born within the mind and a unique clarity illumines and lights up understanding. This light is the wisdom of God. . . and understanding receives this clarity and enlightenment whenever it arises and through its passionate longing penetrates into the union.

In a similar way insight, in the sense of the intuitive power of realization, is developed more and more through *Zazen*, particularly with *satori* and especially if enlightenment is continually deepened.

Let us listen again to what Ruysbroeck says:

The summit of the natural way is the essence of the soul, which clings to God and remains immovable. This essence is higher than the uppermost heavens, deeper than the bottom of the sea and greater than the whole earth with all its elements; for spiritual nature is superior to all physical things. Here is the natural kingdom of God and here the function of the soul comes to an end. For no living creature can affect the essence of the soul; God alone is capable of that, he, who is the Essence of Essences, the Life of Life, the Origin and Supporter of every living creature. That is the way of the natural light, on which one strides forward with the natural virtues and a free spirit. It is called natural, because one makes one's way without the power of the Holy Ghost and without the supernatural grace of God, however, this high goal is only rarely reached without the grace of God.

This description is very positive and shows that the 'way of natural light' can also lead to a genuine mystical experience. At the same time, however, it implies that grace, in fact, plays a part in most cases. Whether the person concerned is conscious of this is another question.

This view, without a doubt, coincides with the enlightenment experienced in Zen, although in Buddhism it would be expressed in different terms. From this we can see that one must be completely free from all sensual imaginings and thoughts (the highest mental functions): *munen-muso*. Then all external attributes will fall away and the emptiness of consciousness, the inner vision or pictureless seeing will arise; for it is only from this state that the higher mystical experiences are possible.

Along the paths of mystical experience and also in Zen training a stage is reached of great peace. However, the Zen masters warn constantly against pausing here, however pleasant it seems, if one's own True Nature is to be genuinely seen into. There is, though, also a peace that is in God and not in the Self. This peace is good, as it is the peace of the path's culmination. Both states, however, are very similar and it is therefore difficult to distinguish between them. A deeply charitable response towards one's fellow men is normally considered a reliable indicator and if this is absent, then it is not the peace of God. On the way to *satori* we continually feel as if we have been abandoned and are lost in complete darkness. It seems impossible to find a hold anywhere, neither among people nor in God. The 'distress' becomes virtually unbearable.

What is a person to do in such a situation? In answer to this question Ruysbroeck outlines three points. 'The first is, that from the outside to be well-ordered in all the virtues and within to be unhindered and free in all external activities, just as if one were not active at all. Otherwise a picture of one's activity is carried around inside oneself and as long as that remains, true seeing cannot arise.' All pictures must vanish from the inner depths and complete emptiness and alertness be present, as before *satori*.

'Secondly to hold inwardly close to God with a burning passion, love and devotion just like a burning, inextinguishable fire. As long as this state is maintained, true seeing is possible.' It is exactly this wholehearted and uninterrupted effort, that must be renewed and purified again and again through meditation.

'Thirdly to have lost oneself in an unawareness and obscure darkness, wherein all those who have beheld God have lost their way . . . in this unfathomable darkness, the

revelation of God and eternal life begin . . .
See this concealed clarity . . . this light is so
great that the devoted beholder of God in
the depths, where he rests, is unable to
perceive or feel anything other than this
incomprehensible light . . .' The Zen
experience encompasses both this obscure
darkness and incomprehensible light. The
second and especially the third part of these
guidelines outline the basic attitude of this
whole instruction, which is essential to enable
a seeing into one's own True Nature.
Whoever is so inclined, whether a Christian or
a Buddhist, will never be disappointed in the
end, but will be richly rewarded for his effort.

Zanmai: Sign of Approaching Enlightenment

Zanmai is the crucial state in *Zazen*. If this state
can be attained by means other than *Zazen*,
then the spiritual effects—the most important
ones—can also be achieved without Zen. The
effects on the body, health and long life,
however, are not such a clear matter. *Zanmai*
could be called a state of deep collectedness
or absorption.

The word itself derives from the Indian
samadhi, or perhaps more correctly: *samayan*.
Even though they were originally pictograms,
the Chinese and Japanese characters for the
word *zanmai* are of little help in explaining its
meaning, as these characters were only
chosen for their sound. The Chinese did not
translate the Indian word, but took it over as
it stands. When writing it therefore, they
chose characters that sounded as close as
possible to the original *samadhi*, although,
inevitably the pronunciation was altered to a
certain degree.

More important than its linguistic explanation, though, is the different usage of the
word *zanmai* in Zen. Here it is not used to
designate enlightenment, nor are there any
clear distinctions made between the various

levels of *zanmai*, although one does refer to a
greater or lesser depth. To begin with there is
still some conscious activity taking place, but
later the 'I' becomes more and more
subdued. This state is not permanent and
at first lasts only during meditation. There is,
however, also a *zanmai* outside meditation.

This state is known to most religions. Zen,
Yoga and certain other methods can lead to
it, but *zanmai* also sometimes appears without
any obvious cause. The late Carl Albrecht,
physician, psychologist and author of such
remarkable books as *Psychologie des mystischen
Bewussteins,* [A Psychology of Mystical
Consciousness] and *Das mystische Wort* [The
Mystical Word] describes this state—without
any reference to Zen—in the following way: it
consists of first detaching oneself from the
outside world, then emptying the consciousness and finally unifying the consciousness.
For this reason this state was also well known
to the Christian mystics.

An example is Augustin Baker, an English
Benedictine monk, who lived from 1575 to
1641. In his early years he had a profound
experience, which for a long time he

neglected. Later on, however, he experienced a second conversion and began again to strive for wholeness. To this end he spent many hours in daily meditation and in the following quotation recounts the method he employed. It is written in the third person and Baker refers to himself as 'our pupil'. He writes:

> In Tauler, Harphius and other mystics we read, that everyone who endeavours to become spiritual must draw his external senses inwards and then raise these inner senses to the superior or intellectual powers of the soul,

where they must finally be annihilated. Thereafter the powers of the higher soul must gather themselves together into their unity, which is the principle and fountain whence those powers do flow and in which they are united. And lastly, that unity, which alone is capable of perfect union with God, must be applied and firmly fixed on God. And now I ask myself, whether what our pupil has told you about his constant exercises, which all strive to draw all the activities of his body inwards, is not the same thing about which the mystics speak . . . I have no doubt, that for our pupil, as well as for all others, the best prayer and the best active contemplation is the complete liberation of the soul from all corporal organs and faculties. It seems to me, that our pupil exercised his will upwards and consequently pulled all that was base after it . . . in my opinion it seems as though he will become more and more spiritual, just as if the soul were operating without the body.

Memory, reason and the will function separately in everyday life. For instance, a decision comes about when one is reminded of something, reflects on it and then makes the decision. Naturally there are also impulsive decisions. When consciousness is joined to this, however, it is a different matter. Then the depths of the soul are touched and acts are not fixed, but born.

In Zen, while in the state of *zanmai*, the consciousness alters in the sense that the inner person withdraws further and further from the outside world, this occurring, however, without any real change in the functioning of the senses. One sees and hears as usual, but one is not distracted by these sense perceptions. Also the sense of pain can alter. Sometimes the pains in the legs, which seemed unbearable but a minute ago, will suddenly disappear. These pains are caused to a great extent by tension and so if, during deep *zanmai*, complete relaxation occurs, then this cause of pain is removed and with it the pain itself. The sense of time can also alter or even to a certain extent be completely lost. One may not notice that time is passing and is surprised when the meditation comes to an end, even though it feels as though it has only just started.

In spite of these remarkable changes, the Zen masters say that we are not really conscious of being in *zanmai*. If we become aware of it and then reflect upon it, it is already left far behind.

Meditative Doing

It may seem even more surprising that there is, as previously mentioned, a *zanmai* outside meditation. This can occur, for example, when one is completely absorbed and concentrated in a particular activity, and in fact, many people have achieved enlightenment in just this way, even though they were unable, despite all their efforts, to achieve it during *Zazen*. In Zen this particular kind of *zanmai* is highly valued.

People who are not permanently resident in a monastery and are also unable to spend much time in daily meditation are encouraged to take part in the main training retreats (*sesshins*) from time to time, as well as to keep up the daily practice—and most important of all—to be concentrated in the doing of every activity, i.e. in eating when eating, and in every situation to give themselves wholeheartedly to the matter at hand; not just physically, but with full mental alertness as well. If one could do this, then it would be possible to achieve enlightenment outside the formal meditation time. Those who try this, though, soon discover that it is easier said than done. It is not possible, for example, to think about merit or honour or anything else and still remain fully concentrated on doing the work at hand. Neither is this meditation to be understood as a pondering of a theme, but rather as an inner attitude. Some people are able to carry this off so well that the work itself becomes their way of relaxation and moreoever they can get by with very little sleep.

This does not mean that one should constantly be thinking about meditation while working and indeed at all other times too. To try consciously to 'meditate' continuously would only serve to split one's attention. Just as it is impossible to be always thinking about God while working. Only a natural grace from God, that enables the work to be done, as it were, of itself, would make this possible. Both Zen meditation and work agree negatively, in the sense that everything superfluous is pared away, and

> *God rests in those*
> *who rest in him.*
>
> Meister Eckhart

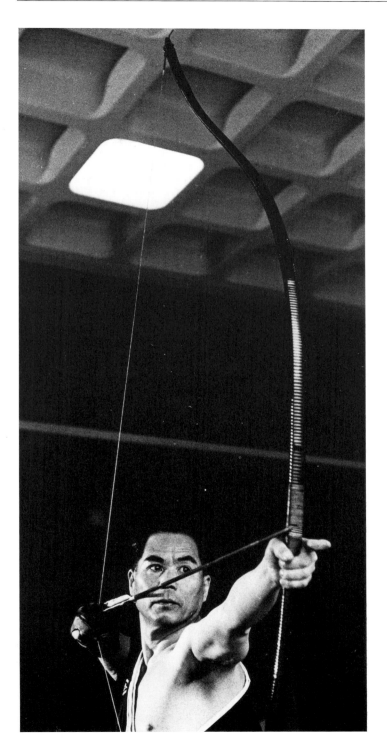

positively in that one should be wholly concentrated on the matter at hand. The difference being that in one case the concentration is directed towards an object and in the other it is without an object. During meditation concentration is an 'unconditional holding on' to that darkness, into which one sees (C. Albrecht). *Zanmai* is an absorption, or a way of absorption, that withdraws from the outside world and empties and unifies consciousness. For this to occur, one must 'let go of all accepted theories, psychological constructions, mere thoughts and judgements' (C. Albrecht). This statement poses two problems: first, the mere thought of having simply to throw away our entire, hard-earned intellectual household causes a great conflict to rise up within us. And second, we shrink back from the idea of throwing ourselves into nothingness. Regarding the first point one can add: it does not mean 'to throw away for ever', but rather 'to put aside'. Some writers, however, insist that attachment to any article of faith makes attainment of this goal impossible. According to this view any specific religious belief is in fact a hindrance.

But this is not strictly true. Rather it means, that during meditation one should avoid consciously occupying oneself with conceptual details. St John of the Cross also expresses this view. It is not a matter of having to throw away one's faith. Zen monks do not do this either. They remain Buddhists, and even during *sesshins*, where *Zazen* is practised virtually all day long, the religious ceremonies are observed at specific times. All of which would be pointless if it were not based on belief.

The Reverse Side of the Spirit

Let us look now at the second problem facing us, namely that of the plunge into nothingness. First of all it must be admitted that this jump is truly a great risk, but at some point a person must take this chance if he or she truly wants to achieve deep *zanmai* or that state necessary for mystical union in the Christian sense. This has always been a difficult point for Christian spirituality and one has always warned against completely emptying consciousness and thinking of nothing during contemplation. This was considered senseless and dangerous, as unwholesome thoughts might penetrate into this emptiness. The Zen masters, however, are very skilful in steering round all these obstacles without any harm. I noticed this very early on and in this sense they are excellent spiritual guides.

In order to get a deeper and fuller understanding of *zanmai* let us examine a Japanese form of expression, which as well as being used in normal everyday speech is also used to describe spiritual phenomena, and that is the distinction between the front side and the reverse side of the spirit. One speaks of the front side and the reverse side of the spirit, which is here synonymous with the heart, and correspondingly of the function of the front side (*yushin*, existing heart) and of the reverse side (*mushin*, no-heart). The first includes above all, conscious activities and dispositions, for example likes and dislikes,

envy and jealousy, the whole range of human passions. In contrast the reverse side contains unconscious activities such as evenness of temper and calm.

In the state of deep collectedness a kind of shift or sudden reversal can take place and all at once agitation completely disappears and a deep calm replaces it. This experience does not occur only during *Zazen* practice, but can occur at any time. Perhaps one is completely occupied with a particular worry and cannot get rid of it, even though rationally it appears completely unjustified or at best useless. Then all of a sudden it appears as though everything has been blown away and a profound calm reigns within. When during *Zazen* sleepiness or strong pain suddenly disappear this too is the same phenomenon. The Zen masters say one does not know one's own *zanmai*. This kind of *zanmai* is the most important on the way to *satori*. Only in this *zanmai* is *satori* possible. It can happen that the sound of the temple bell rings exceptionally beautifully in a hitherto unfamiliar way, as if one perceived all of Beethoven's symphonies in this one sound of the bell.

If in our daily lives we are able to remain constantly in a state of *zanmai*, then it is possible to attain enlightenment at any time or place, even when we least expect it.

Day four
Absorption
Asceticism
Meditational Power
Daily Life

The State of Absorption

We are now half-way through the *sesshin* and must continue our efforts to get deeper into absorption. Please remember that the state of *zanmai* cannot be attained through willpower. The process of absorption itself can be viewed in two stages (see Appendix p. 93). In the first stage, the beginning of absorption, there are still various distractions arising from both outer perceptions and the inner picture-making faculty.

> In the first stage of absorption we find a large number of processes of consciousness and contents of consciousness. These have the character of thought-processes and are experienced as distractions. The second stage contains a state of consciousness that is already to a large extent unified. There are no longer any distractions and thinking has for the most part come to a standstill, that is, there are no longer any long trains of thought or focused developments of ideas. They have become superfluous. (Carl Albrecht, *The Psychology of the Mystical Consciousness*)

In meditation as it is commonly understood, thinking is directed and developed, the nature of meditation being to focus thought and intention. This changes, however, as one becomes more and more absorbed and finally, in complete absorption, meditation is no longer a concentrated act; here meditative thought occurs without any conscious activity or intent. Nevertheless this meditative process has a definite structure. It is directed towards an object, but in a different way from meditation on a concrete object. The seeing within or pictureless seeing is a seeing into darkness, but not a seeing of darkness. It is a seeing in which nothing is seen, but not a seeing of nothing. For this darkness, which is seen into in the process of not-seeing, always simultaneously contains the mystical presence.

Carl Albrecht continues:

> In the profound state of absorption the space of consciousness is empty of all sense perceptions. The few remaining traces of the world of perceptions are experienced as passing reflections and have not the slightest effect on the underlying state. This screening of the world of perceptions and the complete lack of relation to it is an important part of the process of absorption and is experienced as a detachment from the environment.

It is not that the senses cease to function so that, for instance, nothing is seen even with the eyes open, but rather that the sense perceptions remain, so to speak, on the threshold of consciousness and complete peace pervades the consciousness, so that whatever enters has no effect. The sensitive stimuli that arise in the body, such as the pain in the legs that can occur in the beginning, when sitting in the Lotus-position, are also no longer felt as such. Pain is in fact sometimes felt as if it were the pain of another and it always slips more and more into the periphery of consciousness. Such phenomena are signs that one has penetrated deep into the state of absorption. In this meditation the sensatory aspect of the experience is always strengthened in favour of the intellectual aspect, and so feeling increasingly permeates thought.

The consciousness of absorption is not yet completely empty. The Zen masters say of this, that *munen-muso*—the state 'without concepts and thoughts', is not a state where thoughts no longer arise, but where one is not affected by them.

Carl Albrecht says the following about this:

> The emptying of consciousness in the process of absorption does not mean that all experience is erased, but rather that the sole contents of consciousness are streams of experience, which have been stimulated by secondary sources and are thus able to flow out freely, unhindered and uninfluenced by other experiences, as befits their own dynamic energy.

In absorption the consciousness is open to emerging images, notions and other phenomena, which we shall refer to as arising occurrences. *Intuition* is a special form of an arising occurrence. One may suddenly comprehend a truth or a set of circumstances very clearly. This refers to those insights which are spoken of, for example, in the 'Cloud of Unknowing' (see Appendix no. 48) and which arise unexpectedly, even though mystic union has not yet been attained. These intuitive insights are given to those who make a real effort in this kind of meditation without an object, for this practice fosters intuitive awareness and therefore makes the spirit more receptive to the divine light.

Silence is of great value in absorption, even though it is not an arising occurrence. To begin with it has an impersonal quality, beyond any consciousness. Therefore the Zen masters also say: one cannot know one's own *zanmai*. It is the 'Cloud of Unknowing',

In the Far East the bamboo stands for the man of Zen: typhoons can topple even steel buildings and yet the bamboo can withstand all storms. It bows down to the ground and then straightens back up again, unbroken, after the wild storm passes. The secret is the hollow space between the rings. This corresponds to the 'empty heart' of the man of Zen, who like Daruna, the Japanese tumbler-doll, always bounces up again whenever he is knocked to the ground.

through which one must pass. This silence and 'doing nothing' are in no way a waste of time.

The next stage that may arise following absorption is the *ecstatic consciousness*. This indicates the ceasing of the duality of subject/object, which was still present in the previous stage of seeing within. Seeing within does not then become ecstatic, but is dispersed in the ecstasy of the onset of *satori*. This is the first real experience of unity. It is not necessary, as some have maintained, to go into a trance in order to experience Zen enlightenment and the fact that an ecstatic state does or can take place, signifies only that at the moment of enlightenment the duality of subject and object has fallen away.

Whoever wishes to find his True Self, clearly understands that the idea of this Self is a 'primal value' of his life and that the encounter with this 'archetype' within absorption is an extremely valuable experience.

This corresponds to the rule for spiritual discrimination: everything disruptive of the soul's peace is seen as negative and all that cultivates its peace as positive.

The Essential Turning and Looking Within

The mystic Johannes Tauler followed a practical path, namely the way of man's thorough transformation. Accordingly man, who is normally led by the impressions of his senses, should become a spiritual man: a man whose innermost being is permeated and guided by God. To do this he must turn and look within, to the depths of the soul, which for Tauler is the *essential nature, the true heart.* According to Tauler there is a sensual man, a rational man and a third man, 'that is the essential nature, the highest part of the soul, a man is all this.'

This also corresponds to what Tauler says of the image of God within man, which is not found in the three faculties of the soul—memory, reason and will—or in the functioning of these faculties, but in the depths of the soul itself. 'Thus, through the grace of God, this depth of the soul possesses in all its profundity everything that God possesses by nature. Grace will be born to the extent that man allows himself to look within.' According to Tauler, then, God by nature already lives in the soul, but for His grace to benefit the soul in the fullest sense, a turning within is necessary.

In another passage Tauler has this to add: 'The masters say that this essential nature of the soul is exceedingly noble; that it is always active, whether man sleeps or wakes, whether he knows it or knows it not; he has a divine, infinite, eternal inward avenue leading back to God.' This getting-to-the-bottom of things and working through all that lies between is also aimed at in Zen meditation. Even though the Japanese do not know the expression, 'the depth of the soul', they are aware that this path has the nature of man in view; they therefore also refer to enlightenment as 'seeing into one's own True Nature'. Stage by stage the entire path of Tauler's transformation of man has its parallel in Zen.

When should the turning within, as Tauler refers to it, take place? At this point we must be clear that this is a real withdrawal from all perceptible nature, from all imaginative notions and even from our customary thought patterns and contents, just as in Zen meditation. Some of you then may wonder if there is anything left after this withdrawal has taken place.

Nothing! This became clear to us long ago. In Christian asceticism, especially in the Catholic tradition, it is traditional to begin with those exercises that use the sense perceptions, imagination and deductive thought. Tauler also assumes this basis and we find the same view expressed in the above-mentioned 'Cloud of Unknowing'. At some time or other each one of us experiences a crisis, which is a sign that the time has come to look within. This crisis does not befall only those lofty souls with a special

> *Diligent practice*
> *in the end demands,*
> *one should sink down*
> *into the deepest ground.*
> *In those depths*
> *become that nothingness!*
>
> Johannes Tauler

calling to mysticism, but to a greater or lesser
degree all those who have for a long time
practised contemplation according to the
'Way of the Beginner'. The cistern is dried
out. Therefore it is necessary for all those
who wish to continue, to look within.

Johannes Tauler deems it necessary to
'enter into the depths of the soul'. He knows
no exception. This view corresponds to things
as they are, for the transformation of man
must penetrate to the deepest core of his
nature and not remain on the surface.

In his book, *The Dark Night*, the great
Spanish mystic, St John of the Cross,
gives a most impressive description of the
purification of the memory. About this
emptying of the memory he writes, among
other things, that the criticism is often raised
that it means 'the eradication of the natural
application and normal functioning of the
soul's faculties', and that man therefore
becomes 'as wretched as the animals,
for he would be without consciousness'.
Furthermore he would be incapable of

reasonable thought or of recalling the basic needs of life. In contrast to this God does not destroy nature, but perfects it!

St John counters this by saying that the more memory approaches a union with God, the more the individual perceptions fall away, until they finally disappear altogether. This occurs particularly 'when it merges into a state of perfect union'.

Here the saying of St Paul proves to be true: 'He that is joined unto the Lord is one spirit' (1 Corinthians 6:17). 'Accordingly,' says St John of the Cross, 'all the original stirrings of these faculties of the soul are divine. And it is no wonder therefore, that these faculties are transformed in God.' This corresponds to the 'turning' of the medieval mystics, which as we have seen has its parallels in Zen. St John of the Cross's reply to the objection that to empty the memory is unnatural, paradoxical and against God's intended order, applies equally to Zen. That this emptying is only permissible when it is brought about by God himself, does not in any way correspond to St John's teaching, for in this next passage he talks of the active purgation, not the passive one; he speaks of what man himself can do, adding, however, that those efforts alone are not sufficient to attain the high goal of perfect union: 'I must in fact admit, that God must elevate the soul to this supernatural state. Yet the soul too must prepare itself for this as much as it can. And that can happen naturally, especially if God helps as well.'

He also gives practical advice on how this can be brought about. One should strive to forget all impressions of the senses immediately, so that no image of them is imprinted in the memory.

'No picture of recollections should remain fixed in the memory . . . just as if these things had never existed. One should leave the memory completely free and unobstructed and above all do not try to attach it to any reflection.'

For all those who wish to attain *satori*, the Zen masters recommend this very same exercise through the practice of the 'Mu' *Kōan* in daily life.

Asceticism Then and Now

These days it is difficult to find any positive sense in some of the privations undertaken by many of the saints. All ascetic practices have positive and negative aspects, which must be clearly distinguished. Many of the saints died the Great Death for the sake of others and hoped to save other people through this sacrifice. Today, however, we can no longer carry out the more extreme forms of asceticism, because we would soon meet our ruin through them. Nor is it necessary to undertake them now, although certain ascetic elements can be very helpful to us.

On our path of meditation we must also make some mental and physical sacrifices, in order to achieve the goal before us. St Bernard and St Ignatius both had to bear with chronic stomach ailments due to their

frequent fasting, but we should not adopt these extreme forms to purify the senses and the heart in order to bring about a transformation.

The Western distinction between asceticism and mysticism is unknown in Eastern spirituality, at least in theory. Consequently the customary recommendation of asceticism to everyone and the limiting of mysticism to only those who seem to have a special calling for it is non-existent. On the other hand the practice of virtue is considered as a necessary prerequisite for mysticism. Accordingly a gradation of prayer, as St Teresa of Avila teaches, is unknown; the problem of if and when one should give up discursive reflection in favour of another simpler one, does not even arise. On the contrary, the general rule holds, that one should steer clear of all thoughts during prayer: 'Take care, that during the time of prayer you guard the mind against all thoughts, so that it remains steadfast in its calm; then he, who has

compassion with the unknowing ones, will also come to you, and you will receive the glorious gift of prayer.'

The basis for this is the same as for the Western mystics. Because God is very basic and boundless, he cannot be grasped in concepts or mental images. The church fathers knew that detachment alone did not guarantee perfect prayer; consequently if 'the mind does not linger over speculating on things, it can reach the realm of prayer. But if it remains at the level of looking at things that exist, it can get lost in reflecting on these' and thus remain far from God. Therefore they have radically to refuse all images, even virtuous and holy ones: 'If you want to *achieve calm* and be alone with the only God, you should accept nothing that appears to the senses or the mind, neither within you nor outside you; even if the image of Christ or an angel or a saint or any apparition should appear to you. Remain critical and unmoved in the face of such things . . .'

Jōriki and *Chi-e*: Meditational Powers

I would like to speak about two of the effects of *Zazen*, which do not specifically pertain to meditation as such, but which are consequences of it and which form a foundation for the human heart. They are the strength acquired through Zen meditation, in short meditational power (Jap. *jōriki*) and insight (Jap. *chi-e*). *Jōriki* is the ability to quieten the normally distracted mind and establish a spiritual equilibrium and calm. This ability is expressed as the

highest degree of concentration. It helps maintain inner peace and increasingly develops freedom and independence from everything that would normally disturb the spiritual balance. In other words, it helps to contain the emotions and allows the heart to regain its equilibrium with greater ease should the concentration be lost through severe emotional trauma.

This does not, however, give rise to passive indifference and apathy. The contrary is in fact more likely. Zen masters are often powerful personalities. But even among the lay practitioners of Zen one finds strong characters, distinguished statesmen and enterprising businessmen. *Zazen* is beneficial in all walks of life, because it develops a wholehearted concentration on the work at hand. This strength also benefits the religious life in that it cultivates inner collectedness, which is of such great importance for all kinds of prayer, meditation and liturgy. In such troubled times as the present this becomes very meaningful. If someone actually can find time for prayer amidst a heavy schedule of activities, it will be of very little use to them if they are unable to free themselves inwardly from their daily activities during the time set aside.

In fact each person is only free to a very small degree.

A characteristic of Zen meditation is to open one's spiritual vision and reveal the reverse side of our nature, which normally remains unexamined by us. These unseen activities are brought to the fore, into full awareness and eventually enable us to attain inner freedom. This undoubtedly is of great value to us and our fellow human beings.

This occurs because consciousness is emptied and when this happens the unconscious can eventually come into view and finally be understood.

Insight (*chi-e*) is the intuitive side of realization. The development of intuition, which is initially only present as a potential in man, affects all of human life and is of paramount meaning in the religious sphere. It is particularly important, as the attainment of *satori* lies within this intuitive realm.

The meditational powers of *jōriki* and *chi-e* develop correspondingly as the practice of meditation deepens. When intuitive thought supersedes discursive thinking, then the whole Truth will eventually be grasped.

The Conscious and the Unconscious in Daily Life

Zen meditation does not lead to a loss of emotional sensitivity. Quite the opposite: for example when you meditate a lot, your appreciation of music begins to increase and the music itself is experienced in a completely different way, with much more intensity and depth. The longer you practise *Zazen*, the more richly you will experience nature. You will no longer see and hear just with the eyes and ears, but with all the senses and your whole being and with a deep sensitivity. Zen does not kill the senses, only the ego; it lets everything else come to life.

We should try not to allow disturbing emotions to penetrate deep within us. A person who is experienced in Zen meditation will still feel anger, fear, disappointment, etc., just like everyone else, but the difference is that these are not allowed to penetrate into the inner self. In this respect Zen can also promote our health, which is of importance for our daily lives. Earlier we talked about the front and the reverse sides of our nature. In Japan they speak a lot about the 'activity

of the front side' and the 'activity of the reverse side' of the heart, which we would call the conscious and the unconscious functioning of it. For example, when I have to decide what to do and what not to do, there will be reasons both for and against. Having first duly considered the situation and decided for or against it, I then make what I believe to be a free decision. However, after the action is completed, I may realize that my decision was actually influenced more by unconscious attitudes than by my own conscious deliberations. It is often the case that a person's decisions are in fact only one-third free with the remaining two-thirds being made by the 'reverse side of our nature'.

One of Master Harada's pupils, who attained enlightenment during his very first *sesshin* and later became a qualified Zen master, once said to me, that *satori* is the coming together of the front and reverse sides of our nature. As we already know through *Zazen*, the conscious functioning is pushed further and further back, so that one may become more aware of the unconscious, that is the functioning or state of the reverse side. This becoming aware is something completely new and is also experienced as

> *For whom the day a burden is*
> *and the time drags by,*
> *let him turn within to God,*
> *where time no longer lingers*
> *and all things are at rest.*
>
> Meister Eckhart

such. To begin with the student penetrates into this region of his nature only after great effort and only then for a short time before returning to the front side. If he continues to practise diligently though, it will eventually become easier, until the moment finally comes, when both sides come together. This is, according to that master, seeing into one's True Nature. Those who experience this generally feel an at–one–ness as never felt before. As far as it goes this explanation does not actually deviate from the general experience, but this master also warned, that the awareness of the 'reverse side' might easily be imagined. Often people believe they have attained this state, when they enter the state of *munen–musō* (without ideas and thoughts). However, the awareness that is meant here, goes far beyond that. It is an intuition.

After this talk let us end the day with a prayer:

> Almighty God, listen to our morning prayer, heal the sickness hidden deep within our hearts. Through Heaven's pure grace we were reborn, no bleak desire shall obstruct our way or cloud your image in us.

Day five
Reflection
Mystical Realization
Origin
The Absolute

The Discursive and the Intuitive

Today we shall take a closer look at the different types of perception. Typically the characteristic intellectual function is the ability to progress from one perceived fact to another, so-called discursive or deductive thought. In this way intellectual understanding is constantly on the move, pressing forward from the manifold and random nature of things to their essence. This type of mental activity is seen in the sciences, philosophy and also in daily life. The use of the intellect in this way is common to all people and is always freely available for use at any time.

In contrast the intuition grasps the truth with one simple glance without any preliminary discursive examination. Therefore intellectual understanding is to the intuition as movement is to rest, acquiring is to having, and as becoming is to being. The intuitive function is therefore more complete than the intellectual function. However, with human thought intellectual understanding is the usual mode of operation. This is because man is not pure spirit, but a spirit that is very closely bound to the body. Man's mental activity is therefore closely tied to his sensual nature. Even our concepts arise only through the assistance of the senses. In the same way man must push from one truth to the next. From earliest youth onwards our entire upbringing and education operate along these lines. All our practical and theoretical knowledge is acquired in this way. Our schooling, university studies, and personal experience are all evaluated on this level of intellectual understanding. All scientific endeavour is accomplished primarily through this intellectual function. There too one pushes from one perceived fact to the next. It is different, however, with pure spirits, angels, for example. With them intuitive perception is the primary and common mode of operation. Yet man too does possess this intuitive capacity and in certain instances it is his normal mode of perception. This is true of the so-called primary principles (*prima principia*), for example the principle that something can be considered simultaneously to exist and not to exist. These principles are grasped without any process of deduction from one truth to another. They are understood intuitively and as such need no proof. And yet no science can manage without them, and in fact assumes them to be self-evident. They are like (door-)hinges, without which no scientific system is possible.

The different ways in which intellectual understanding and intuition operate correspond to the difference between their respective contents. Intellectual understanding focuses on the individual, the difference and the distinct, whereas the intuition focuses on the whole; its mode of operation is non-differentiated. In Buddhist terms the world of differentiation (*sabetsu no sekai*) is associated with intellectual under-

---

Stop now, where are you running?
For Heaven it lies within;
If God you seek outside you,
Forever you will miss Him.

Angelus Silesius

standing and the world of sameness (*byodo no sekai*) with the intuition. Or put in another way: individual existence is the object of intellectual understanding, and undivided existence itself is the object of intuition. That is why intellectual understanding deals primarily with the physical element of being and the intuition with the spiritual element of being, in particular the highest absolute being. Human awareness evolved from the physical-sensual to the spiritual-existential.

From these differences we can already see that, as regards their content, there is actually no sharp dividing line between intellectual understanding and intuition, but rather a gradual transition from one to the other. Nor would one expect it to be any different, for intellectual understanding and intuition are not two different abilities, but different ways of the functioning of one and the same ability; the ability to perceive. What is the relationship between the intellect and intuition? St Thomas of Aquinas almost sounds like a Zen master when he answers in the following way: 'Rest is the origin as well as the goal of all movement, for which reason that which moves arises from out of that which rests and similarly returns or flows back into it.' In Zen one would simply say, 'Rest is movement, movement is rest.' Applying this to intellectual understanding and intuition, one could say that intellectual understanding (movement) arises from intuition (rest) and finally leads back into it, or at least it should. In this way intuition is the primary function and intellectual understanding something derived from and subordinate to it. In practical terms this would mean, that intellectual understanding of the thing perceived is not yet a complete understanding of it. This corresponds to our earlier comment concerning these two modes of perception, namely: that intellectual understanding leads to a becoming, hence differentiation (*sabetsu no sekai*), whereas intuition leads to being itself, the undivided whole (*byodo no sekai*). In conclusion, then, we can see that each individual intellectual insight into the true nature of things must be further perfected through intuition, in order for it to become a true spiritual possession. In the same vein Thomas Merton says, 'Every science must therefore be aware of its limits and must be filled with a longing for a living experience of reality, which remains inaccessible to speculative thought on its own.'

Reflection and Meditation

When one talks of Christian reflection or meditation, it usually refers to a kind of reflective prayer, a type of dialogue with God, Christ or the Saints, out of which a certain understanding is gained and is then followed up by a further period of reflective prayer, which is then prayer in its truest sense. This kind of reflection or meditation is at present the most common type practised in Christianity. But if one speaks of meditation in Eastern religions, in Hinduism or Buddhism for example, then something completely different is usually meant. In Zen for instance, where *Zazen* in fact closely corresponds to Christian reflection, the words meditation and reflection are never even used.

However, it would be a mistake to believe that reflection as described above is the only kind of reflection common to Christianity. Ignatius of Loyola makes the following distinction in his Spiritual Exercises: Consideration (*consideratio*), reflection (*meditatio*), contemplation (*contemplatio*).

This division is still valid today in the strict mystical sense of: reflection, meditation and contemplation.

We must realize that there is no clear-cut distinction between reflection and meditation, not even a furrow as between two fields. The transition from one to the other is gradual, with overlapping at the boundaries.

On the same basis that intellectual understanding and intuition were distinguished, we can also view the difference between reflection and meditation. In reflection it is above all the conscious thinking Self, the intellect, that functions in its characteristic way of thinking discursively or deductively, simultaneously with the activity of the sensual imagination. Due to the nature of the intellect a subject/object divide is always maintained. Obviously this determines the nature of reflection, that primarily involves the intellect, and consequently this type is referred to as objective reflection (see Appendix no. 46).

In contrast, meditation, as we understand it today in the real sense of the word, functions through the power of intuition. In

accord with its nature intuition works without a division into subject and object. In its depths the subject/object split is absent, rather the (one) being becomes aware of itself. Therefore this type of meditation, involving primarily intuitive power, is called super-objective. It grasps the Self, the truth, at a single glance. This cannot be truly understood as long as one continues to try and understand it with the intellect. For the intellect divides, whereas the intuition is a unity. In attempting to give a rational explanation, what is being explained is lost. It is like trying to grasp the air with one's hand—it escapes (see Appendix no. 47).

Because meditation involving the intuition lacks a differentiated object, its main focus is the spiritual, in particular the absolute spirit or it is contained by this absolute spirit.

In fact there is a much more intense spiritual activity in meditation than in reflection, where the intellect is the main tool. It is wrong to think of the content of meditation as something we are face to face with. Even if the content or 'object' of the meditation is the absolute spirit, God, it is still not understood and experienced as something the human spirit comes face to face with, but rather as something that the human spirit merges with, as all Christian mystics will confirm.

Absolute Emptiness: The Way to the Absolute

In Zen meditation we must strive to eliminate our discursive way of thinking. For the Absolute, which we yearn to understand, eludes all boundaries, all concepts and all forms of verbal expression. For this reason the East, and in particular Zen, employs a negative mode of expression. One does not speak of the Absolute, but of absolute and perfect emptiness. This is only truly understood through practical experience; definition alone serves only to circumscribe, restrict and differentiate, whereas the Absolute itself transcends all these boundaries and contradictions. When we try to understand God conceptually or make a picture of him, then we do not really understand God himself. In the first commandment we are already taught not to create graven images of God, because the image of God is not God himself. In the Zen experience as well as in Christian mysticism, absolute and undivided being is actually experienced. The difference between the two lies in the fact that in Zen it is a *non-personal* and in Christian mysticism it is a *personal* understanding of the Absolute. In each case the experience is registered so differently that one feels there must also be an essential difference in the phenomenon itself. This difference can be attributed to the respective outlook, tradition and culture of each, but even then the question remains, whether that explanation suffices to clarify the dissimilarity. Even though it might be correct to regard the non-personal experience of the Absolute as the primary one, one cannot at the same time assume that the

Christian experience within a personal context is not genuine.

For among the Christian mystics this element of the personal is so intimately bound up with the experiencing of the Absolute, that it becomes united with it into an indivisible whole. If one were to remove this part, one would not be able to acknowledge the experience as genuine. And not even a Zen master with little knowledge of Christian mysticism would deny that.

In Search of the Spiritual Origin

All mysticism strives for man's wholeness, not in the sense of a theoretical understanding, but as a direct experience. In Zen this wholeness is identical with being itself, that which is immanent in all things, but needs to be brought into consciousness. In the Christian tradition, as for instance in Meister Eckhart, it is the wholeness of man with God; this can never therefore be viewed as an identity, although Eckhart, in fact, pursues it as far as is possible without actually asserting an identity. Where then does this wholeness between God and man occur? Eckhart answers: It takes place in the very depth of man's soul, when this merges with the divine primeval origin. Just as man's eternal Self was born out of this primeval source before taking on body and soul, so the spirit of man must return to this divine origin. In order to grasp this to its full extent, it is necessary to understand that according to Eckhart's teaching this divine source lies much deeper than the divine beings themselves, who actually come forth from it as the manifestations of the one Godhead. And likewise the faculties of the soul, its essential nature, will and spirit, all come forth from the depths of the soul. Further to this, the provenance of God is the place where the Godhead conceals itself as the fountainhead of all persons, spirits and things. Accordingly Eckhart teaches the necessity, for the sake of the Godhead, to leave God. Conversely Eckhart also says of the depth of the soul, 'In all truth and as sure as God lives: God himself will never and not for a single moment look into it (into the depth of the soul); nor has he ever looked in, in as much as he exists entirely in the manner and quality of his own being; for this singular Oneness is without manner or quality. Therefore should God ever look into it, he must lose all his divine names and his personal singularity.'

Eckhart goes as far as saying that the entire Godhead merges into the depth of the soul and that likewise we can work together with God to bring about the birth of the Eternal Son. To understand this we must know that according to Eckhart, man's journey from the eternally concealed Self is this birth from out of the provenance of God.

> *We shall never rest,*
> *until we become,*
> *that which, in God, we have always been.*
>
> Meister Eckhart

Thus this Self emerges, which as the eternal idea of God is itself something divine and 'through the bond with the soul's universal spirit, it becomes for a time a man in this form designated as a body'—this is completely analogous to the becoming of man through the Logos. Because of this it is exposed to the sensual world with all its impressions and consequently the 'imprint of the world and the flesh' is stamped on to the personality. In other words: the eternal Self becomes an empirical Self. Therefore 'the first task of mysticism is to cut off all attractions and impulses of this external world in order that man may become, in a paradoxical sense, a spirit already departed from this world. Only then can the first restructuring of the personality begin.'

In Zen one would say: the completely enlightened being no longer rests on any external moral code, but naturally does good and refrains from doing evil, out of the very depth of the Heart.

One should perform all one does without a *why.* The Silesian Baroque poet Angelus Silesius captured this mystical experience perfectly in his *Cherubinischen Wandersmann*: 'The rose asks not why; when she blooms, she blooms and she pays herself little heed, asking not whether she is seen.'

This 'Without why' parallels the 'Without aiming' of Zen archery (*Kyudō*). Here the archer does not consciously aim and yet always hits the centre, just as for Eckhart, the spiritually complete pauper always acts appropriately without asking 'why'. Naturally both cases assume that the man has already attained perfection. Accordingly this level can never be achieved through practice, but rather comes about of its own accord.

Comparison: Christian Mysticism and Zen

To conclude today's *teishō* I would like to present a table that summarizes and compares the most important similarities and differences between traditional Christian mysticism and Zen-mysticism.

The Christian Tradition	The Zen Tradition
Asceticism	
—*Negative*: Striving for control over the passions and faculties through detachment. —*Positive*: Strengthening and perfecting the virtues. —Example of Christ is emphasized specifically for Christians. —Own effort, at all times including the help of grace.	—*Negative*: Complete detachment (*gedatsu*). —*Positive*: The same. —No complete counterpart, but natural virtue is highly valued. —Own effort.
Meditation	
—Initially at least with an object, especially Christ or the gospel.	—From the start without an object, however, utilizing such means as concentration on the breath and *kōans*.
Mysticism	
—Christian mysticism based on actual experience. —Experience of faith gained through the manifestation of complete Oneness. —Special experience of God as a person. —Essential phenomenon: grace of contemplation from the creation and incarnation.	—Likewise with Zen mysticism. —Experience of being, also experience of faith, in which complete Oneness should be experienced. —Special experience of the Absolute, but not as a person. —*Satori*: Grounded in human nature.

Cause of the Experience

—Grace, including natural inclination (*potentia oboedientialis*): 'Original revelation' as ability 'to hear the Word'.

—Not possible by one's own strength.

—Principally: own, natural powers; none the less, Bodhisattvas (beings that have attained Buddhahood) are called upon; also passive in the sense of an 'acquired passivity'.
—Fundamentally possible through one's own strength aligned with the Absolute.

Preliminary Stages for Seeing into One's True Nature

—Curtailing the activity of the intellect.
—Affective prayer: dialogue with God.
—Simplication of the affects to one single affect, sustained and focused on God.

—From the start no activity of the intellect.
—Prayer to the Bodhisattvas.
—Complete emptiness of consciousness (*munen-muso*).

First Effects

—Attained contemplation.
—Renunciation of all worldly things.

—Lofty conception of God's perfection, actually felt, not just thought.
—God in all creatures.
—Understanding, love.

—Deep joy and inspiration.

—Corresponding to *zanmai*.
—Radical purification from all attachments to worldly things: not differentiated.
—Heightening of the powers of concentration and awareness.

—Openness, understanding, compassion towards all sentient beings.
—Peace and calm, but not inactive passivity.

Dangers and Illusions

—Worry about time lost, because not doing anything concrete in the worldly sense.
—When one gives up the usual object-bound reflection, one loses an important means of perfection: the reflection of sin, of virtue and the example of Christ.
—Through this one should learn gradually to give up the human way of thinking and to think in the way of God.

—The same in Zen—years of effort.

—In Zen there is no object present, right from the start, nevertheless one finds that the tendency to do evil is diminished and virtue is strengthened.
—One sees no danger, provided that one does not get caught up in arising thoughts and pictures.

Christian Contemplation—Eastern Seeing into the True Nature

—Contemplation through grace.
—Simple, loving approach to God, whereby the soul, absorbed in love and admiration, directly recognizes God and, in a state of deep peace glimpses Him as eternal bliss.
—Different from acquired contemplation. Passive, given.
—Not the result of discursive thinking.
—Experience of perfect union.
—Pure spiritual activity.

—Corresponds to *satori*.
—Great similarity, except no personal God: development of awareness, intuition, glimpse of eternal bliss (*nirvana*), able to see with the 'single eye'.
—Here essentially different from *zanmai*. Likewise experienced as given.
—Likewise.
—Likewise.
—Likewise.

Psychological Explanation

—Occurs in the depth of the soul or at the peak of the soul.

—Likewise, but different designation: deepest cosmic consciousness.

Dogmatic Explanation

—Goes beyond faith.
—Through the gifts of the Holy Spirit, God's self-communication.

—Likewise.
—Does not apply here. The explanation goes back to the contents of the Sutras or other scriptures.

God will come to you much sooner,
if you will but stay completely still,
instead of searching for him wildly,
till body and soul fall ill.

Angelus Silesius

With One's Own Eyes

Do not cry, that it is so far away. If you think, that in order to see and hear it, you have to cross the seas to distant China and India, then you can moan all you want that it is so far away. Is anything closer than looking at the heart with the heart, the eye with the eye?

Zen master Hakuin (1685–1768)

The New Consciousness Beyond the Common States of Consciousness

Only through contemplation does one arrive at this new consciousness. In whatever way Western reflection proceeds, whether through intellectual analysis or though the intensi-fication of emotional states, it always remains on that level of the intellect, the senses and the imagination. If meditation is begun with the aim of a deeper frame of mind, then this original impulse can at some point practically disappear and the person may feel that they have, so to speak, reached the centre of the self. In reality this is all just in the head on the level of intellectual understanding. This points to the fact that the *a priori* cause, which underlies the original impulse and out of which it and the subsequent intellectual activities arise, has not yet revealed itself. It has not even arrived yet. It is then said: the Self only appears beyond the perceptible conditions of the consciousness, both the psychological and the moral. According to the experience of the great searchers for the Self, the way to the Absolute only begins after going beyond and leaving behind the ordinary acts of the conscious Self. Perhaps the people of the Graeco-Latin tradition and of the spiritually impoverished modern West would never have had the opportunity of gaining such a clear picture of the inexpress-ible experience of the Absolute and the True Self, had not the East emphatically offered the West such positive evidence of an entire culture, which spiritually belongs to the richest in the world. I refer here to the Indian culture with its many spiritual traditions from Yoga to Zen. It is very difficult to give an abstract description of all this as the Absolute lies beyond the conceptual level. The Zen masters were always aware of this and warn against the temptation of trying to explain the mystical experience completely with words. This can only lead to misconceptions. The culmination of meditation, the experiencing of the Absolute, cannot be put into words. And therefore please understand that this attempt to explain the difference between Western mysticism and Zen, using key terms, is but a rough approach to the reality.

Day six
Mustering up Strength
Purification
Enlightenment
Further Practice

Mustering Up Strength Before and After Enlightenment

We are approaching the end of the *sesshin*. Some people may be experiencing a certain tiredness, but nevertheless everyone should try to continue practising with wholehearted effort. Some require more time than others on their way to enlightenment. Even those who have the greatest difficulties will attain deep enlightenment when the time is ripe. The time that passes until then is never lost, as each person learns many worthwhile things on the way. Never lose your determination!

In general Japanese Zen masters do not discuss their enlightenment experience. There are, however, a few valuable exceptions. Kosen Imakita, for example, relates his experience in the following way:

One night as I sat absorbed in meditation, I suddenly fell into a strange state. It was as if I were dead and everything had been totally cut off. There was no longer a before or an after and both the object of my meditation and my Self had disappeared. The only remaining feeling was that my innermost Self was completely filled by and at one with everything above, below and around me. An infinite light shone within me. After a while I came back to myself like one risen from the dead. Seeing, hearing, speaking, movements and thoughts all seemed completely transformed from what they had previously been. As I tentatively pondered the truth of the world and tried to make sense of the inconceivable, everything was at once understood. It appeared to me clear and real. Without thinking about it, overjoyed, I began to throw my hands into the air and to dance around. Then suddenly I cried out: one million sutras are as but a single candle before the sun. Wonderful, truly wonderful.

Thereupon Kosen wrote the following poem:

Indeed, we have not seen one another for a long time, Confucius! Whom shall I thank, that I was allowed to meet with you in such a world?
But no, it was I myself who found the way here.

Thomas Merton's description of entry into the mystical experience points in this same direction: 'In that moment the consciousness of our false everyday Self falls off like wet and muddy clothes. The deeper Self, lying too deep for consideration or analysis, is then liberated and falls into the abyss of God's spacious freedom and peace.'

The way to enlightenment runs in the opposite direction to the development of discursive thought. It leads back to the state just before thinking arises. At this point one understands that it is necessary to put away discursive thought, in order to arrive at the experience of one's own existence, *satori*. Everything that was acquired along the way must be rendered null and void. All outward attributes must drop off, to allow a new life to arise. The teaching of dying and being reborn is also known in Buddhism, particularly in Zen.

The Immortal Value of the Body: Against Duality

It is stressed repeatedly in Zen that one must let go of everything. If this is taken too literally, it can sometimes lead to a type of spirituality that fails to acknowledge the body as a fundamental part of man.

Contrary to the tendency of Western thought to separate body and soul, the Eastern traditions make no clear-cut, radical distinction between them.

In overcoming duality, the world of opposites, one must strive at all times for unity and wholeness, and this includes the unity of body and soul. The body is physical in the sense of that form with which a surgeon is concerned when he operates, and which decomposes after death. Body and soul, however, suggests a wholeness, something endowed with the spirit of life.

The soul, though, must never be confused with the pure spirit. On the path of Zen meditation we try with great effort to get from the outside to the inside, from multiplicity to unity and to the complete purification of the faculties.

God is a pure Emptiness,
not touched by now and here;
The more you strive to reach him,
the further he recedes.

Angelus Silesius

Along the Labyrinthian Paths of Purification

The way to enlightenment is a way of purification, a way of cleansing. It is always difficult, because on it nothing can be avoided. There are no shortcuts and one will not be allowed to fool oneself for the sake of personal convenience. No self-deception is possible along this way and everyone who walks it will encounter different problems. At various points along the way there will be times when one is forced to face very painful realizations about oneself. Examples of this can be found in the 'Cloud of Unknowing' and various other religious texts. Many of the desert fathers and hermits had to face such shocking realizations.

The Syrian monk Isaac of Nineveh (AD 500–50) is a particularly impressive example of this. He divides the contemplative way into three stages: purification, enlightenment and unification. He also speaks of the apparitions and visions that may appear to the over-zealous worshipper and of the manifestations of demonic forms—those phenomena corresponding to *makyō* in Zen meditation. Even in those times, when considering these phenomena, there was a great emphasis on distinguishing between the spirits.

Isaac's comments on the phenomenon of tears are particularly pertinent for the comparison with Zen:

The inner man stands without fear, as long as he still lacks the fear of tears . . . for once the flood of tears has begun, the spiritual man's labour pains begin. Through the grace granted to all, the soul has been impregnated, that it may secretly bear the divine form for the glory of the future world. And when the time does come, that it should give birth, it begins to stir

in the soul, and drawn by a hidden strength the child steps from its mother's womb . . . And the stronger it grows inside, the richer is the profusion of tears, and the eyes become like a waterfountain. So it goes on for two years or more. Until finally one arrives at the tranquillity of thoughts, at that state of calm, of which St Paul speaks.

This obviously refers to man's natural response to the fruitful inner transformation taking place before enlightenment. This phenomenon of tears also often occurs in Zen before enlightenment, especially over long *sesshins*. Many people, especially Buddhist nuns, speak in their personal accounts of the tears of repentance (*zange no namida*). In Zen too a catharsis, a purification, must take place before enlightenment is possible.

One's first enlightenment experience is usually relatively shallow and so the Zen masters repeatedly emphasize the need to continue to practise even more diligently immediately following this initial attainment. There are very few people who manage to achieve absolute wholeness in a relatively short time. It is best to refrain as much as possible from talking with others about enlightenment. Sometimes when one has been told of a certain person's enlightenment one may wonder why he still seems to have many weaknesses. It is simply that this particular person has not yet reached the goal.

Often the way to enlightenment is compared to a labyrinth. Some of you may have already in fact experienced this. If this way has been traversed once and everything has been truly let go of and a certain depth attained, then there is no going back any more. Certain experiences have occurred that can no longer be forgotten. At the same time a point may have been reached, where one simply does not know how to continue. One is no longer sure whether one is striving towards the light or not. One is in fact taking a genuine risk. On the other hand it should be pointed out that no effort is ever in vain. All that is required for eventual success is to continue consistently on the path. One should never relinquish the Great Faith as only this will help in finding the way out of the labyrinth to the goal.

BODHIDHARMA, born in Ceylon in the sixth century AD, crossed the sea to China (Canton) and is considered to be the founder and first Patriarch of Zen in China. For nine years he practised solitary *Zazen* in the mountains.

Comparison: Christian Contemplation and Zen Enlightenment

In a similar way to yesterday, I would like to conclude today's *teishō* with a table, using key terms, to compare Christian contemplation and Zen enlightenment.

In the Christian Context	In Zen
Calling	
—God's intention: the grace of contemplation in granted, so that man may himself become whole, perform greater tasks or bear suffering. —Contemplation is not essential for bliss. —It is questionable whether every person has a calling to contemplation. —According to the records within the tradition, very few actually achieve contemplation. —Signs of the calling: ● One can no longer reflect in the usual way. ● One finds joy in being alone in loving attentiveness with God, without any particular consideration for oneself.	—Enlightenment too is primarily a means to bring man to wholeness, which should also express itself in service to fellow human beings. —Enlightenment is necessary for final liberation and deliverance. —Because enlightenment is necessary, everyone has a calling, whether in the present existence or in a later one. —The number of those who attain enlightenment seems to be relatively greater. —No signs necessary.
Longing	
—Longing for contemplation is permissible, provided there is humility and a pure intent. However, if it arises through pride, then contemplation is hindered and the person will lose his way. —There is an inner longing, that cannot be satisfied in any other way; one should follow it with pure intention.	—Every Zen-Buddhist should long for enlightenment, but if this longing is grounded in pride or is disorganized, then it becomes a hindrance. —This applies to enlightenment as well, and one's intent must likewise always remain pure.

Extra-ordinary

—Do not strive for visions and the like in mystical experiences.	—Do not strive for visions (*makyō*).
—If in spite of this they do arise, one must remain inwardly detached.	—Likewise.

Levels

—Incomplete contemplation 1st stage: concentrated prayer. faculties turned within. Less distraction, but ecstasy.	—This is included under *zanmai* 1st stage: *zanmai* at advanced level. Likewise.
2nd stage: quiet prayer. calm, peace, joy, not ecstatic. Initially short, later longer. 3rd stage: intoxication of love.	2nd stage: *zanmai* at a higher level. Likewise. 3rd stage: no equivalent, except perhaps to feel mystically moved.
—Perfect contemplation 1st stage: mystical union.	—*satori*. 1st stage: corresponds approximately to the little insight (*shōkenshō*).
● Complete withdrawal and the unification of the respective faculties. ● Transformation in God.	● Likewise in seeing into one's True Nature, including the little insight. ● Transformation (*jōbutsu*) i.e. becoming Buddha.
● Communion of the soul with God in the manner of the pure spirits. ● Of short duration, but prolonged effect. ● Loss of the I-consciousness.	● Here too, pure spiritual activity. ● Likewise. ● Likewise.
2nd stage: ecstatic union, i.e. the activity of the external sense perceptions ceases.	2nd stage: *satori*, not normally associated with ecstasy and never rated higher just because ecstasy arises.
3rd stage: completed union, also called marriage.	3rd stage: great insight (*daikenshō*) Designations such as marriage not recognized in Zen.
● Clear sight of the Trinity. ● Short duration, but the influence of divine persons remains. ● Afterwards no further hindrances in practical life.	● Clear sight, but not differentiated. ● Also short, the effect remains, though undifferentiated. ● Likewise.

A gradation as in Christian mysticism is not usual in Zen.

Trials

—Up to perfect contemplation.
● Spiritual dryness.
● Demonic temptation, especially threatening one's faith and other divine and moral virtues.

● Retrospective doubt about the authenticity of the received grace.

● Mystical purgatory, as for example in the 'Dark Nights' of St John of the Cross.

—Up to great insight (*daikenshō*)
● Likewise.
● *Makyo* and especially the temptation to give up *Zazen*, as one loses courage and trust to attain enlightenment. Through *Zazen* faith grows and combats these doubts.
● Doubt about whether anything has any value or use. Received grace is not mentioned in Zen.
● Complete purification is essential and can be very painful, an equivalent of purgatory.

Signs of Authenticity

—Not comprehensible or discursive.
—The taste for sensual pleasures becomes spiritualized, in that one experiences God in the beauty of His creations.

—Always striving to deepen one's perfection.
—For verification, seeking the judgement of the spiritual guide.

—Likewise.
—Heightened sense of joy. To a certain extent one experiences with the whole being, not just with a single sense, such as the eye, etc.
—Likewise.
—Authentication by a Zen master goes without saying.

Effects of Perfect Unification

—Deep sustained peace.
—Longing for suffering, in order to become more like Christ.
—Humility, remaining conscious of one's own sinfulness.
—Ardent and pure longing for the honour of God and the salvation of one's fellow men.
—Inexpressible joy.

—Likewise.
—Does not apply; however, strength to endure suffering.
—Humility, gratitude and the consciousness of the fact that one must continue practising.
—Strong desire to help others on their way to enlightenment.
—Likewise.

How Shall I Continue?

I am frequently asked by the people taking part on these *sesshins*, 'How do I now continue to practise alone?'

The most important thing is to find a time and a place when and where you can meditate regularly every day. The secret of progress lies in this regular practice. Taking part in a *sesshin* from time to time is not enough to sustain the effects of meditation.

A story is told of a priest who took part in an ordinary devotional course. Sometime later someone asked him about the effects of these devotions. In reply the priest said, 'It was wonderful, and this time it was a whole month before I was back in the old rut.'

Therefore keep up the practice. It will be sufficient if you practise 30 to 40 minutes daily. Choose the best time for yourself—morning or evening—a time when you can meditate undisturbed.

When you have once decided to walk this way, stick with it and continually trust the guidance of an experienced master.

There are nowadays always more new groups forming in many cities, where one can practise regularly with a group (see Appendix, p. 93 ff).

Day seven
Satori
Fear of Death
Ripeness
Experiencing God

Enlightenment: A Point Where Speech Ends

I would like to devote this last day of our *sesshin* to the most important goal of every Zen student: to *satori*. Moreover, I would like to draw your attention to my book, *Zen Meditation für Christen* (hereafter referred to as *Zen Meditation for Christians*) (Munich, 1976), where the meaning of *satori* for Christians is discussed in great depth. In fact today I will also refer mainly to this text (pp.56–68) in the closing discussion of this inexpressible reality. However, please do not forget, that this is only an attempt. You should, though, be able to get a certain feel for it from this.

When you develop a deep feeling of oneness and peace through *Zazen*, this is not yet enlightenment. At this point many people allow themselves to be misled by an overwhelming sense of joy and they stop practising diligently. Our life's problem, the great matter of life and death, cannot be solved through concentration alone. It can only be solved through enlightenment and the subsequent integration of this experience. So even if we want to free ourselves from the fear of suffering in this life, our main concern in *Zazen* must be the experience of enlightenment.

Zazen and enlightenment are not meant to make you a strange, eccentric or esoteric being. Rather you should become a normal, true, and as far as possible whole human being. And now a quote from my book:

> *Satori* or seeing into one's own True Nature is the highest experience in Zen, the goal, so to speak, that *Zazen* strives towards. This does not mean, however, that following the attainment of *satori*, there is no longer any need for practice. Consequently although *Zazen* should lead us to *satori*, it does not mean that we have reached the goal with that; for *satori* is not a permanent state. It must therefore be constantly renewed, again and again, until an ethical perfection has also been attained. Only when a person reaches this state, is he or she truly enlightened. And so it is constantly stressed, that one must continue to practise after the attainment of *satori*. On the other hand, once this breakthrough has been achieved, the practice of *Zazen* becomes more effective than ever before.

What then is *satori* or seeing into one's True Nature? According to the findings of all those who have experienced it, it is in fact something inexpressible in words. Zen masters therefore either refuse to answer this question or else they reply in such a way that the answer becomes a *kōan*, which can only be understood when one reaches enlightenment oneself.

Every Day is a Good Day

It is easy to endure the unendurable, if you think, that it will last but one day. It is the same with pleasure: if you consider, that it too will last but one day, then you will not cling to it.

Zen master Shōju Rōjin (1642–1721)

Sri Ramana Maharshi: Deliverance from the Fear of Death

Instead of listing accounts of *satori* experiences, I would like to present just one case from India that seems to be particularly helpful in this connection. It concerns Sri Ramana Maharshi (1879–1950), born in Tiruvannamalai near Madura. I always tell his life story again and again (here quoting from my book, *Zen Meditation for Christians*), because it contains all that is essential for *satori*:

> His experience occurred when he was a 17-year-old student at college. Although by religion a Hindu, he had not done any particular training along these lines, nor had he shown any exceptional piety or desire for mystical experience. He was—or so it seemed—just a normal student of the college. This college in Madura was run by American Protestant missionaries. At the time Maharshi and his older brother lived with an uncle. One morning Maharshi was suddenly overwhelmed by the thought that he would soon die. It engulfed him with a tremendous intensity and filled him with a great fear. Nothing had happened in his surroundings, that could explain the cause of this thought and such fear. Soon his whole consciousness was filled with the thought: I could die, I will die. I am a 'being for death'.
>
> His reaction, however, was not to try and rid himself of this thought of death, as one might have expected of such a young and lively boy. Instead he took the challenge on, looked the possibility of death right in the eye and decided to pit himself against it. So he lay down on the floor and imagined that his life was withdrawing from his limbs, one after another, and as death was approaching closer and closer to the most essential parts of his

body, his eyesight, hearing and sense of touch were disappearing, and his thoughts were clouding over, the flow of thinking was beginning to stop and the consciousness of Self disappearing, right up to that moment where one enters the state of sleep.

Then just at the moment when his consciousness disappeared, as it abandoned him, so to speak, there arose of itself with supreme and liberating clarity and intensity the consciousness of existence itself. Everything had disappeared without a trace in the face of this overwhelming consciousness of: 'I am.' Neither the body, the senses, any thought, nor ordinary consciousness, which could have conveyed this experience, remained. There was only this experience bursting through, flashing forth, arising of itself, radiating with its own unique clarity, free of any hold or tie: 'I am.'

It was a pure light, that dazzled like the midday sun and did not allow any differenti-ation of details. Everything was filled with its radiance. Everything appeared only in this radiance. There was nothing left except this radiance.

Along with everything else, death too had disappeared. For what kind of death could still touch one, who simply *is*, one whose whole consciousness is consumed in the single awareness of *Being* itself? External things— whatever they may be—and similarly too the senses and abilities that manifest themselves through this consciousness of being, may change and disappear. But the one who *is*, elevated above all these comings and goings, does not change and does not disappear. He remains; for he *is*. He who can say, 'I am,' exists on a plane of reality, that no threat or destruction can reach.

Maharshi's experience was indeed a wonderful *satori*, the traces of which could in no way be erased. All that remained was for it to ripen completely and pervade his entire being. This Maharshi cultivated. He gave up his studies, retired to the sanctuary of Arunachala and became a Sādhu. After staying at the temple for several months he moved to the neighbouring mountains, where he stayed for the rest of his life and became a great sage. He never sought the company of others, nor concerned himself about pupils. But he did not turn away anyone who sought advice from him. And indeed many came to him. Yet he taught no specific method, just the way of paying attention to breathing in and breathing out. He left everyone in peace. The only thing he ever insisted on, was that one should discover who one truly is: what is there in you, that remains independent of all the changes in body and soul? Maharshi had discovered this himself in his profound experience: the true 'I' or Self, and that one should look for nothing else. Everything else is meaningless. If this one thing is found, then all other problems dissolve; as long as this is not found, these problems, which actually need to be cleared up, never come to an end.

Moon In The Water

When human beings attain enlightenment it is like the moon reflected in the water. The moon appears in the water without getting wet and the water is not disturbed by the moon. The light of the moon covers the earth and yet it can still be contained in a small pond, in a little dewdrop or even in the tiniest drop of water.

Zen master Dogen (AD1200–53)

For Ramana Maharshi death became a *kōan*, a burning problem, that filled him with fear and distress. With this *kōan*, though, he reached enlightenment. He did not try to avoid it. In the instant when his entire consciousness was filled with this problem, was then emptied of it and died, the solution came: 'I am.' This indicates a direct self-awareness. Not the awareness of the empirical I, but of the ultimate and deepest Self, which is immortal. This is, according to its content, also the essence of *satori* in Zen.

In Zen one often speaks of man's 'original form'. Expressed in the form of a well-known *kōan*: 'Before your mother and father were born, what were you?' This self-perception is an intuition of the Self and is therefore also called 'seeing into one's True Nature'. Everything that stands in the way of this intuition must be cut off. Therefore the emptying of consciousness has to take place. The experience of Ramana Maharshi may serve to testify to this.

The Experience: Oh, that is how I am!

Even the best description of *satori* remains incomplete without the personal experience itself. For this reason we must always look to the traditional mystical writings in which this experience is presented in more or less successful imagery. Yet Carl Albrecht has brought a new aspect to light on this question:

> The contemplative stands face to face with this vast darkness, out of which the bolt of lightning strikes in the moment of ecstasy, which is at the same time the deafening thunder. His seeing is not only blinded by the brilliance, but is also completely obliterated by it. Experience no longer occurs through seeing. The lightning flash marks the end of seeing and strikes not only the beholder, but his very wholeness as well. This wholeness is the vessel containing the non-distinguishable experience of suffering both as an awareness and a sensing, as well as a perception and a feeling. As seeing is overwhelmed it becomes blinded by what was hidden in obscurity.

This pictureless seeing 'is a looking into that darkness, in which nothing can be perceived, and yet there is present in this darkness just that which the contemplative is searching for. Seeing is thus a conditionless adhering, an incomparable, direct adhering, undisturbed by any picture.'

In Zen enlightenment, too, there is that ray of light that breaks forth out of the darkness. There are various degrees of depth in the description of enlightenment and similar mystical experiences. But in all these, it is always a leap into something totally new and never a gradual change from what went before. However, this new state is felt with varying degrees of intensity. In the case of Maharshi and some of the great Zen monks, it was like an explosion that threatened to shatter their very being. Such powerful experiences do actually still occur in Japan today, occasionally even to lay Buddhist practitioners. These people, however, prefer not to speak about it.

Once, at the very beginning of my Zen training, I asked a Zen master, whether enlightenment is in fact an intuition. He replied, 'That is just an interpretation.' Another time I asked Harada Rōshi what the difference was between a great and a little enlightenment. He promptly replied, 'You do not need to know that at this time.' And of course he was right.

Later I asked Mazuda Rōshi, the novice master in the same temple, whether enlightenment is an intuition. He replied, 'No, *satori* is ethical perfection. The perfection of man.' That man attains perfection when truly enlightened is indeed fitting, but it did not really answer the question of whether the experience is an intuition or not.

The third person I approached with this question was a much practised lay follower who had also attained enlightenment, and he said, 'No, not an intuition—it is a new strength.' From a slightly different perspective it can also be seen as: a kind of experience of the true Self. Not, however, through a tremendous bursting forth as Ramana Maharshi experienced, but more as the Japanese say: *kigatsuku*—Oh, so that is how it is! That is how I am! One is astonished that one did not realize this before, and one is also deeply moved. This, however, must not be confused with enlightenment. The intensity of emotion is not a reliable indicator of genuine enlightenment. It can in fact vary greatly. For example, it may be very tranquil around me, but nevertheless a true enlightenment may suddenly arise. Conversely it may be a very powerful experience, yet still have nothing to do with enlightenment. A very powerful emotion may disappear as suddenly as it arose, leaving nothing behind. Only a genuine enlightenment remains.

The Inherent Energy in the Experience of *Satori*

For a long time now I have pondered over what exactly is meant by this manifestation of powerful energy in *satori*. In this connection I would like to quote again from my book, *Zen Meditation for Christians*:

In trying to understand this energy it may be useful to consider the following. In man the power of perception, which we looked at earlier, along with all other spiritual activity, is normally associated with the sensitive, affective aspect of human nature. This aspect readily arises from the interrelationship of body and soul, the nature of which is such, that to separate them would mean certain death. But the awareness arising from enlightenment is a purely spiritual awareness: that is, it functions independently of the sensitive aspect of man's nature.

This would imply that the spirit, in order to function freely, must be separated from the body and thus become detached from the sensual realm, or to put it another way: man must for a moment, at least, die, for this to come about. The relationship between body

and soul is not meant to be understood in the sense of the soul or spirit living in the body as in a house. Rather this relationship is of such a closely interrelated nature, that it cannot be grasped with a material image. For this reason too psychology also avoids speaking of the body/soul relationship in this way, regardless of any bias against the religious. The denial of this clear-cut body/soul division is also implicit in Buddhist teaching, and therefore in Zen too. If in spite of this the spirit is meant to function independently from the body, then the actual relationship between them must be broken up; they must be torn apart. Looked at in this way, the vigorous energy mentioned in some *satori* experiences is more easily understood.

This also helps us to understand why, in Zen *sesshins*, it is repeatedly emphasized that one must be willing to die and indeed must die, if enlightenment is to be attained. If anything at all is still clung to then the necessary leap of consciousness will be hindered.

Naturally the genuineness of a *satori* cannot be judged solely by its vigour. Man cannot be compared to an electrically charged body, whose behaviour can be predicted in advance. Even if every genuine *satori* is an insight into the True Nature, it does not mean that the nature and strength of every case will be the same. I emphasize this here in order to prevent any misunderstandings. Sometimes this 'leap', this transition occurs in a much more gentle way than in the examples cited above. In that case the Zen master will scrutinize the experience and perhaps wait to see if it repeats itself. Or he may give a different *kōan* and see how the pupil responds, before acknowledging the *satori* as genuine.

In fact he will often not acknowledge it, even though he believes it to be genuine, in order to make the pupil continue practising with all his resources. It is also true that those who take many years of diligent practice to attain *satori* have a more profound insight than those who take a shorter time. The natural disposition of each pupil plays a large part in this, even when the effort and the practice are the same.

The Assessment of *Satori*

Who determines whether a *satori* is genuine or not? And who is actually able to attain *satori*? Let us continue to read from my previously mentioned book:

Satori must always be assessed. Generally speaking it is easier to do this in instances where the trainee has been practising for a longer rather than a shorter time, as then more has already been achieved through long training. The cumulative effects of *Zazen*—for example, moral transformation, meditational strength and insight—are thus more developed and also the *satori* itself is usually deeper. This brings us to another question that is frequently asked: how long then does one have to practise to reach *satori*? This has actually already been answered or at least hinted at: it is not possible to specify a definite number of days, months or years. It is also true to say, that in the present day the majority of Zen monks do not attain *satori*.

This may astound some people, but perhaps the term monk is a little misleading here. In this connection we usually think of people who have lived a life of strict discipline and celibacy within a monastery and have spent many hours a day in meditation. But this is no longer the case in Japan, nor has it been for a long time.

Since the Meiji period all Zen 'monks' have been allowed to marry and indeed today also most of them do so. A large number of these monks inherit their father's temples or the official position at these temples. The son then lives in the temple with his wife and children and ministers to the religious well-being of the families within the temple parish. As well as the various social duties encumbent on this position, he must also carry out the material and administrative management of the temple. Therefore he lives very much in the 'world' rather than in solitude. In these circumstances the life of a monk, as we normally think of it, is not possible, and if the monk has not yet attained enlightenment, he is even less likely to now. In fact it often happens that the monk gives up daily meditation altogether.

> *In God no thing is glimpsed:*
> *he is a single whole.*
> *What we perceive in him,*
> *indeed, must be ourselves.*
>
> Angelus Silesius

Nevertheless the possibility of training to attain *satori*, with a high likelihood of success, does still exist in Japan today for those who are willing to devote themselves wholeheartedly to *Zazen*. In this context the percentage of those who achieve it is relatively high, and this also applies to laymen who practise diligently and regularly and arrange their life-style accordingly.

The guidance of a Zen master is also a very important factor and consequently good Zen masters are sought out by those wanting to attain enlightenment, even when it means travelling great distances. Such masters have no need to advertise, nor do they do so.

But perhaps a more important question than this is whether enlightenment is actually necessary for everyone or not. There is no doubt that the practice of *Zazen* is of great value for everyone, enlightenment aside. But it is also correct to say that the experience itself is of a great worth. There is also an element of personal temperament to consider here. There are people who at some time feel a very strong yearning to attainment enlightenment at any cost, without even understanding what it is. Their motive is not ambition, but rather a deeper reason for concern. These people, in spite of all their involvements with family and work, always find time to make use of every training opportunity and tend to attain their goal with relative certainty.

Then again, others may well feel a need for this kind of meditation and perhaps even think about enlightenment as a distant goal, but at the moment they do not feel that inner yearning to reach it at any cost. These people should not, however, feel obliged, as it were, to strive for enlightenment on the basis of theoretical consideration, but should just learn meditation, practise it regularly and always try to let the meditational attitude penetrate their everyday life. Although these people certainly do not have the same likelihood of attaining enlightenment as the former type, it is not altogether impossible that one day they may attain *satori*, when they least expect it. They do in fact have one advantage, and that is that they are not preoccupied with the thought of *satori*, which can indeed be a real hindrance towards achieving it.

Moreover, it is also true that some people cannot achieve achieve enlightenment despite their diligent efforts and seemingly favourable conditions. The Zen masters say, of course, that everyone can achieve *satori*. This is certainly true if it means that this potential is inherent in all men and women. And yet there can be hindrances, especially in the individual disposition, which in spite of the best intentions cannot be completely overcome in one lifetime.

Satori: The Way to Human Maturity

Even after the first experience of *satori* and its authentication by a Zen master, there is still a long way to go: the assimilation or integration of enlightenment. Following this one no longer talks of enlightened or not-enlightened, for these differences are now superfluous. It may then be, that one has to do things that others cannot understand or easily accept. Nevertheless, one must do them. It is still possible to find such people in India today, where many face radical decisions which can completely change their previous way of life. With regard to this, let us return again to my book, *Zen Meditation for Christians*:

Ever since ancient times it has been the custom in India for a man first to marry, start a family, raise his children and help them to become independent, and serve society through his work. Then, after completing all this, he begins a totally new life. He becomes a Sādhu, a religious mendicant, who even in conditions of extreme poverty is concerned only with spiritual progress and perfect liberation. It is the way of the holy man, a way still highly respected in India today.

This way of life is certainly not possible in all times, much less in all places. But there are certain ways in all times and places, that can lead to this final perfection and everlasting liberation; and all they require is the courage to walk them. In this very respect Zen is one such way, especially when followed to *satori* and then further still to its complete integration and utilization. At the moment of enlightenment it can be said that the coloured glasses of delusion fall off, or as it also has been put, all outer forms fall off. However, even if we do not succeed in reaching this experience, the glasses at least become more and more clear through the emptying process of *Zazen*. Just the knowledge of the coloured glasses itself can spare us many a hasty and wrong judgement. And even after attaining *satori* great care must be taken to prevent the glasses from gradually becoming coloured once again. *Zazen* with or without *satori* is a way leading to greater inner freedom.

At times of crisis when one realizes that one is not free after all and serious doubts about oneself begin to arise, then one can no longer find a hold on what one always believed was one's own. A difficult choice must then be faced: there must either be a complete inner surrender of everything and a single-minded striving towards the final and absolute reality; or else, one must take hold of something else that is not yet this final and absolute reality. The latter, however, would be a great mistake.

Nevertheless, most people do in fact settle for such a choice, and they may, sooner or later, even find a certain peace in that, but a great opportunity will have been lost for ever. For the rest of their lives they will remain unfulfilled, not only objectively and absolutely, but also subjectively and relatively. In other words, they will not only be imperfect in the sense that all men, even the most holy, are, but also in relation to the potential they could and indeed should have realized personally. That potential is different for each person and everyone should strive to attain the level of perfection that is personally possible. Only to the degree that this level is approached will happiness and peace, that is truly real and enduring, arise.

In addition to reaching this peace there will also be an inner freedom that allows one to act in the manner most appropriate to a situation, without any noticeable difficulty or inner restraint, at least as far as one's potential allows. This has a great meaning for one's relationships with others, because it is not just a matter of a peace that brings only personal happiness, but one that allows one to contribute more to the happiness of others than is otherwise possible. People who thus achieve their true potential are—or become—those most able to realize the 'mystical thinking' we discussed before. This is because they now lack all prejudice and are therefore clearsighted and able, as far as is humanly possible, to grasp the truth. All things and all people are seen as they truly are.

So far we have spoken mainly about the ethical aspect of *satori* and it goes without saying, that this facet of seeing into one's true nature can be of great benefit to Christians as well as to Buddhists. This purification, this catharsis of all that is 'amiss' or is a hindrance to a higher awareness, is of great significance in all religions, including the Christian one.

Man, while in this world,
if time and tide do seem too long,
Then turn yourself within to God
into the everlasting now.

Angelus Silesius

Satori: The Way to the Experience of God

There are many people today who—although called Christians—have never truly experienced Christianity. On the other hand a non-church-going Christian, who is able to observe the Christian faith with deep reverence, may spontaneously experience *satori* as a realization of God. In this context it has often been asked: does *satori* have any

meaning for Christian belief? For the answer to this let us again look at my book, *Zen Meditation for Christians*, where this question is dealt with in depth:

We have already answered this question positively in the sense, that Zen meditation can make Christian belief easier and also reawaken faith, where it has been lost. But here the question is posed from a slightly different perspective: whether the experience of enlightenment itself can enrich the content of our faith? Sometimes it is also asked, why the Buddha and the great Zen masters did not find their way to the belief in God, despite their deep enlightenment. Hence the question about the relation of *satori* to the belief in God.

The question of whether the Buddha believed in God or not is in fact somewhat controversial. It does seem certain that he always maintained a silence, when asked about God, the soul or the life to come, but that alone does not prove that he did not himself believe in God. One could cite other reasons for this silence and in any case there are also people in India today who hold the opinion that the Buddha did believe in God. Mahatma Gandhi, among others, readily comes to mind.

Whether the Zen masters ever came to a 'declared' belief in God can initially be answered with a 'no'. There are, of course, exceptions, but they are rare. However, Zen Buddhism is not atheistic and the Zen masters, or at least most of them, would certainly reject any claim of its being so. This would seem to be a contradiction and in order to clarify it, we must examine the question without the use of sharply defined concepts.

It would seem, that in spite of everything Zen enlightenment is in a certain sense an experience of God. Indeed, it is true that there is hardly a Zen master today who would talk about enlightenment in this way, if only for the reason that it implies a duality, and Buddhism denies all duality: everything is one. We can, however, leave the word 'God' to one side for a moment and say without hesitation that enlightenment is a 'realization of being'. In trying to understand the meaning of this realization more clearly we must ask ourselves what exactly it is, that is here being realized. Is it a relative state of being? To the Zen Buddhist this would be meaningless and would certainly not constitute a seeing into one's True Nature; for in Buddhism one strives to transcend this relative being, and as far as the Buddhist is concerned it has no ultimate reality, as we have in fact already seen. For him, regardless of whether he would call it this or not, or whether he even sees Nothing or Emptiness, seeing into the True Nature is an experience of absolute being. It is the absolute and ultimate reality [. . .]

Conversely, it is therefore easily understandable that a Christian, when granted enlightenment, feels it to be a direct experience of God [. . .]

The difference between the Buddhist and the Christian attitude towards this experience is often characterized as the contrast between the absolute 'It' and the absolute 'You'. I, too, would like to add a comment to this which I hope will lead to a better understanding of this problem. I would like to quote from the words of someone, who has been living in India for a long time and has penetrated deeply into the mystical depths of Yoga:

'As long as man has not yet gone through the all-consuming experience of the simultaneous nearness and remoteness of "being", can it really be to God that the "Thou" of his prayer is addressed? Does he not thereby run the risk of stopping at but a mere reflection of the truth, which he assumes in the mirror of his soul, or has grasped in his thoughts?'

God is not a 'Thou' like a man is an 'I'. His 'Thou' is infinitely far removed from the human 'I'; it has no limits and is beyond all concepts. Therefore there is no question of being allowed to enter into a dialogue with God. Did not Christ himself teach us: 'Our Father, which art in heaven, Hallowed be *thy* Name!' But we should always remember that as long as we live, we are for ever on the way to God and must always continue to search for Him, because we can always find Him more perfectly, even if we no longer have any doubts at all about his existence. He is only truly found, completely and perfectly, when He is no longer seen as in a mirror, but beheld face to face.

To remind ourselves again, *satori* itself is a direct perception of the True Self. Now this in no way contradicts what has just been said, because from here there is also a way to God. For the True Self is of a spiritual nature and lies deeply rooted in the original ground, which in fact is God. Therefore this True Self can be perceived directly without reflection, but not without reference to the absolute Being [. . .] It has been verified again and again, that when man arrives at this deepest Self, he finds God. At this point the Self is then dissolved and consequently the Buddhist experiences a complete at-one-ness or non-duality.

With these inspiring pointers let us end our *sesshin*. This is also to be found in Christianity: there, when a man is completely at one with God, he does not just stand next to Him, but rather they simultaneously lie one within the other. As far as one can possibly imagine that . . .

In fact no one can possibly imagine that. It is no longer 'I' who lives, but 'It' that lives in me. This then is the truly fully enlightened man. At least as far as is at all possible in this life . . .

Appendix
Exercises
Illustrative Material
Glossary
Information

The Way to Correct Sitting (*Zazen*)

The Zen master will only accept those pupils with some amount of training to attend his *sesshins*. During a *sesshin* one is expected to be able to sit in the Lotus position or, in most cases, in the Half-Lotus position for up to 13 half-hour periods, that is 6½ hours a day, over a period of 5–7 days. At first this is a difficult challenge, particularly for the body, but it is also one of psychic endurance. The meditation position, which is second nature to those who practise daily and have been training for a long time, is difficult for the beginner and requires hours of strenuous practice. Although there are some meditation centres that also offer training for beginners,

it is advisable and necessary to begin practising the Zen meditation position oneself. The later one starts the more sensitive the pains and the stiffer the muscles will be. Almost all children, and those individuals who have practised Yoga for longer periods of time, manage the Full Lotus position effortlessly. A 40–50-year-old adult requires about 3 to 6 months of constant daily practice to be able to hold the Half-Lotus position for 30 minutes. Making use of the easier forms of sitting is, of course, tolerated in certain exceptional cases, but it slows down the progress of true Zen meditation and makes it more difficult. Therefore, before resorting to the more modified sitting positions, it seems sensible to exercise daily, in order to enhance the elasticity of the muscles. One should practise these exercises for about 15 minutes in the morning and again in the evening, as well as doing them for 10 minutes before and 5 minutes after sitting, altogether incorporating about 45 minutes into the daily routine. In this way one can prepare oneself for a real *sesshin* before applying to a Zen master. After the first *sesshin* this daily habit of practice will have become more familiar, strengthening and consolidating the meditational experience and helping to maintain one's constancy as a Zen pupil.

> *I will sit*
> *and be silent*
> *and listen to*
> *God's voice within me.*
>
> Meister Eckhart

> *When someone practices* Zazen, *even if only for 20 minutes, it is as if the whole world were practising* Zazen.
>
> Zen master Dōgen (AD 1200–53)

Loosening and Stretching the Hips and Thighs

After a few warming up exercises (neck roll, stretching the arms, legs, waist and spine), one proceeds to more specific exercises, which help to develop correct sitting.

1 Stretching the inner thighs: bend the knees down to a squatting position, place the hands on the floor behind the feet, rest the inside of the knees on the elbows and then gently rock the hips a few times.

2 Loosening the inner thighs: place the hands on the floor between the knees and the feet, push the inner thighs apart with the elbows and rock the hips to the right and to the left.

3 Seated on the floor: firmly hold the shins and press the knees down with both elbows. First alternate the sides and then stretch both legs apart at the same time.

4 Lying on the back: bend the knees and with the hands pull them towards the trunk.

5 Open the knees sideways, grasp the feet and press them gently downwards.

6 Stretch the legs out sideways, grasp the ankles and gently push downwards a few times.

Stretching the Whole Body

Seated on the floor, raise both hands upwards.

Exercises 7–19 may be harmful to anyone with injuries to the spine and joints—take professional advice first!

7 Bend one leg in, leave the other extended, then stretch the trunk upwards.

8 Bend the trunk over the extended leg and pull it down with the weight of the arms, rest the forehead on the knee. Hold for 1 minute—return to starting position —change sides—hold for 1 minute again.

9 Spread legs wide apart holding the shins, keep the knee creases on the floor and hold the trunk upright.

10 Bring the trunk and the head down to the left knee— return to starting position—change sides—hold for 2 minutes.

Abdominal Rocking

After a short rest to loosen up, lie down on the stomach.

11 The forehead rests on the floor, the legs are brought
    up to the buttocks and the feet are clasped around the
    outside of the instep.

12 Arch the back into a bow and rock on the stomach for
    30 seconds. Breathe deeply through the nose in
    rhythm with the rocking—then relax.

Rocking on the Back

Sit on the floor.

13 Lift the legs up and hold on to the toes.
14 Rock back and forth on the spine, from the buttocks to
    the shoulders.

15 Breathing exercise—while breathing in roll on to the
    shoulders and while breathing out roll on to the
    buttocks—30 seconds.

The Shoulder Stand

Lie on the back.

16 Breathe in and swing the legs over the chest, propping
    yourself up with the hands.
17 On breathing out gives the legs a swing backwards
    and lift the hips off the floor.

18 Support the back with the hands in the lumbar region
    and bend the legs over the head.

19 Let the hands slide down the back as far as possible,
    stretch the legs and the back upwards. Hold this
    position for 2 minutes and breathe deeply through the
    nose.

Sitting Variations and Correct Posture for Zazen

Now practise correct sitting: In all sitting positions the buttocks are pushed out, the spine is held upright, the hands remain close to the body resting on the thighs or the heels, the knees lie on the mat, the abdomen is relaxed, the head is held erect and the eyes remain open, focused on a point on the floor about 90–100 cm away.

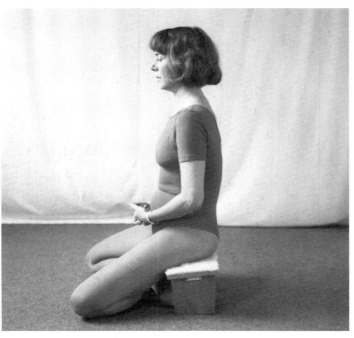

20 To start with use a low *Zazen* bench: this should be approx. 45 cm long, 17 cm wide, approx. 20 cm high at the back and 13 cm high at the front; possibly upholstered or covered with lambskin. In order to get used to a 30-minute sitting period, it is advisable for the first week to start with the heel- or Quarter-Lotus position on the *Zazen* bench (see also no. 23).

21 The traditional support for *Zazen* is: a round cushion, 30–45 cm in diameter, 7–15 cm thick, filled with Kapok, the Malayan padding material, and a ground mat approx. 5 cm thick and 90 × 90 cm large.

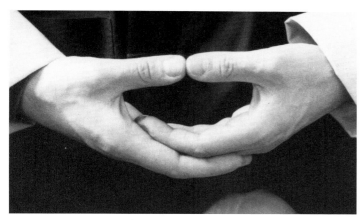

22 Place the hands, palms facing up, one in the other. The thumbs are held horizontally and their tips lightly touch.

23 This Japanese posture, known as the Diamond-seat, is the proper position during the interview with the Zen master (*dokusan*): kneel on the mat and place a support cushion between the heels and the buttocks (except when using a low bench), to ease the weight on the heels. The cushion is 40 cm long and 6 cm thick and is filled with the husks of buckwheat, rice or other grains.

The Lotus Position and Modified Zazen Positions

Do not give up trying to achieve the proper *Zazen* posture, the Full Lotus position, throughout the long months of persistent exercising.

24 *The Full Lotus position* is the ideal *Zazen* position: both feet are crossed and rest on the opposite thighs, the hands rest on the heels.

25 *The Half-Lotus position*: one foot lies on the opposite thigh, the other foot rests under the opposite thigh.

26 *The Quarter-Lotus position*: one foot lies on the thigh of the opposite leg, the other foot lies under the opposite leg. For the Half– and Quarter-Lotus positions it may be necessary to use a support cushion (or if need be at first the low *Zazen* bench, see no. 20), so that the knees can rest on the mat more easily.

27 *The modified Lotus position*: sit on a low stool, cross the feet, the tips of the toes resting on the floor, the heels raised.

28 *Position on a chair*: the chair should have a straight back and a firm seat; use a cushion if necessary, so that the knees are lower than the pelvis and the feet are placed firmly on the ground.

Relaxation after Zazen

After practising *Zazen* for 30 minutes in the morning and 10 minutes in the evening, it is necessary, particularly for the beginner, to massage the stiffened foot joints in order to overcome the pain:

29 After a *footmassage* (joints, arch, *sole*, and toes), lie down on the floor.

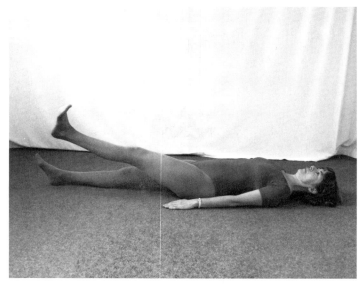

30 First lift one leg at a time, then both together and stretch and rotate the feet around the ankle in both directions.

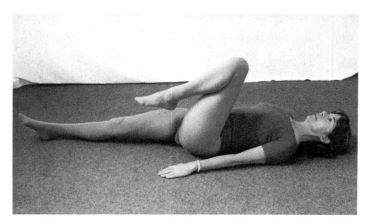

31 After approx. 30 seconds take up the *bicycle-position* with toes pointed. Raise each leg off the floor alternately, bending one knee and straightening the other leg.

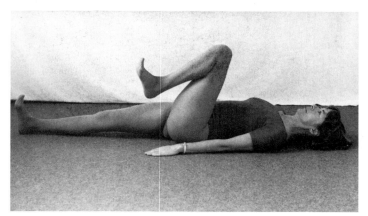

32 Bend both feet up and repeat the previous exercise.

33 Seated on the bench: with clenched fists firmly tap all the muscles, from the buttocks to the soles of the feet and all around the legs.

34 Starting from the thighs, now tap all the remaining muscles down to the ankles.

35 Finish these relaxation exercises off by beating the soles of the feet and then do the following exercises in supple walking.

Relaxation in Walking: Kin-hin

During Zen *sesshins* approximately 10-minute-long breaks are introduced between the *Zazen* sitting periods. During these breaks *kin-hin*, a special kind of walking to relax the limbs, is practised.

37 Put down the left heel and simultaneously lift the right heel.

36 Starting position: form your left hand into a fist enclosing the thumb; place the fist on the solar plexus, knuckles facing up, the lightly arched right hand enclosing the back of the left hand, the forearms forming a horizontal line; direct your gaze approx. 3 metres on the floor in front of you.

38 Transfer the weight on to the ball of the left foot and raise the right foot completely.

39 Raise the right foot for the next step and while putting down the right heel, lift the left heel at the same time, and so on.

The Way to Correct Breathing

Along with correct sitting, Zen meditation is strongly moulded by correct deep breathing. Just like sitting with crossed legs, deep breathing is for most Europeans a question of tedious practice. Breathing through the *mouth*, with its corresponding breathing from the *chest*, has become a bad habit of our times, which results in a variety of physical deformities. Apart from this it also makes it more difficult to penetrate to the deeper levels of man.

Breathing through the *nose*, and the corresponding *abdominal* or *deep* breathing that results, has an essentially different structure from breathing through the mouth. The constriction and angularity of the nasal passages effect a slowing down of the in- and exhalations and also make the breaths deeper and longer. Whereas a one-year-old child needs *c.* 35 breaths per minute, an adult in a state of relaxation takes between 14 to 20 breaths per minute, and an experienced practitioner of Zen meditation merely needs 6 to 10 breaths per minute during deep or abdominal breathing. Correct breathing is best practised during the daily sitting by observation or by counting the number of breaths taken.

Observing the Breath

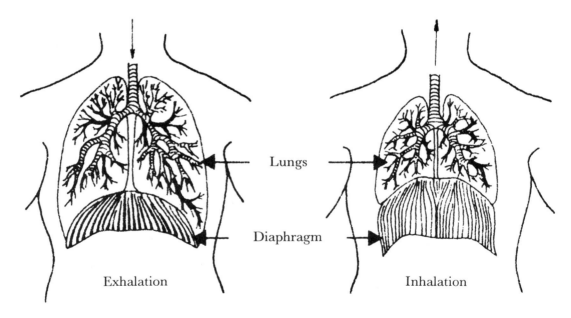

Lungs

Diaphragm

Exhalation   Inhalation

40 During inhalation: clear the head of its burden of thoughts and focus the entire attention on the stomach, feel and control the increasing depths reached.

41 During exhalation: do not pause, but release the air evenly and out of the depths breathe away everyday thoughts. Observe the disappearance of all distractions.

Counting the Breath

The most reliable way to breathe correctly is to count the number of breaths from 1 to 10. This can be done repeatedly whenever it is convenient.

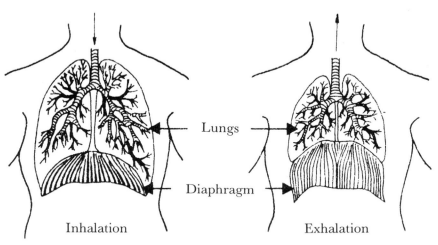

Inhalation   Lungs   Diaphragm   Exhalation

42 Breathe in on the odd numbers:
   1   3   5   7   9   1 . . .

43 and breathe out on the even numbers:
   2   4   6   8   10   2 . . .

Counting Inhalations

Counting Exhalations

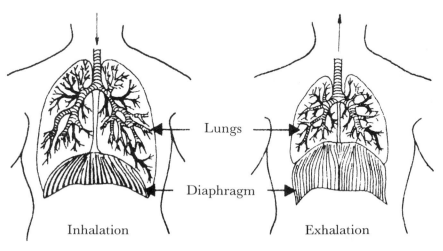

Inhalation   Lungs   Diaphragm   Exhalation

44 When thoughts are particularly intrusive it sometimes helps if one counts only the inhalations and ignores the exhalations:—an aid against distractions: 1 to 10, and again 1 to 10, and so on.

45 On the other hand, if one becomes sleepy, which is not an infrequent occurrence during 'not-thinking', one should count only the exhalations and ignore the inhalations:—an aid against sleepiness: 1 to 10, and again 1 to 10, and so on.

The Way to Correct Inner Collectedness

A helpful way for Europeans to approach correct inner collectedness is by becoming aware of our Western traditions and knowledge. In doing so it is important first of all to be clear about the essential difference between discursive reflection and intuitive meditation.

The Structure of Discursive Reflection and of Intuitive Meditation

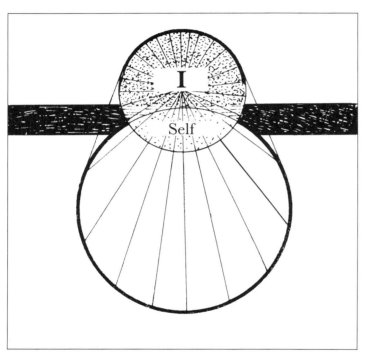 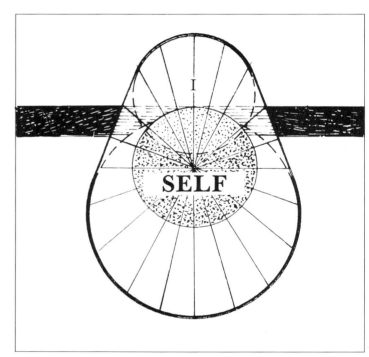

46 *Reflection* is top-heavy and concentrates on an object, thus establishing a duality: I and the object of perception. The Self also becomes an object of the Ego.

47 Intuitive *meditation* abandons the Ego and concentrates on the Self, which is focused on the Absolute outside of consciousness. If the Ego is not integrated with the Self, then it can become a distraction.

The Structure of Meditation According to the 'Cloud of Unknowing'

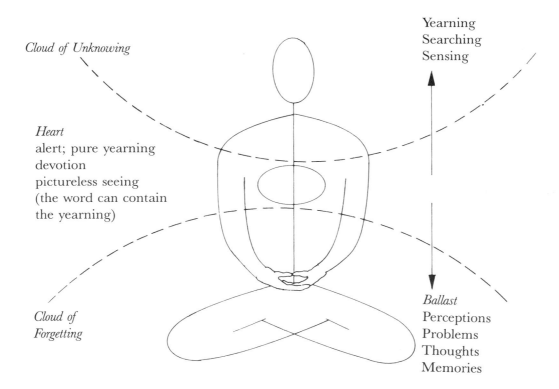

Yearning
Searching
Sensing

Cloud of Unknowing

Heart
alert; pure yearning
devotion
pictureless seeing
(the word can contain
the yearning)

Cloud of
Forgetting

Ballast
Perceptions
Problems
Thoughts
Memories

48 The sketch above encompasses three realms, the realm of the *base* (the Cloud of Forgetting), the realm of the *summit* (the Cloud of Unknowing) and the realm of the *heart*. The meditator should dispose of all ballast, such as perceptions, problems and thoughts, under the *Cloud of Forgetting*. The spiritual process of forgetting is associated with the physical base of the body, thus producing a strengthening of this base which, similar to the *Mu*-breath of Zen, facilitates an upright, yet relaxed sitting position.

Rising upwards the meditator should enter the *Cloud of Unknowing*, that is, the sphere of his or her consciousness should remain open and free. Through physical alignment upwards, the posture of the meditator too stretches upwards, almost of its own accord.

The meditator should penetrate into this cloud with the *yearning of spiritual devotion, with the whole heart*. For

God cannot be grasped through thoughts, rather He is embraced in loving devotion. All activity during meditation is therefore twofold: a *detaching* and a laying aside of everything peripheral, and a *striving towards* the ultimate reality from the centre of the person, from the whole heart.

Should the beginner find it difficult to maintain this spiritual yearning after God and to stick with it, it is suggested that he or she enclose this 'cloud', this yearning, in a short word, like keeping it in a container. Then the beginner can hold fast to this yearning more easily and through attentiveness to the word containing the yearning he or she can screen off all the distractions brought on by perceptions and thoughts. This methodical aid is related to the Indian Mantra-meditation and to the Jesus-prayer of the Eastern Church.

The Process of Absorption

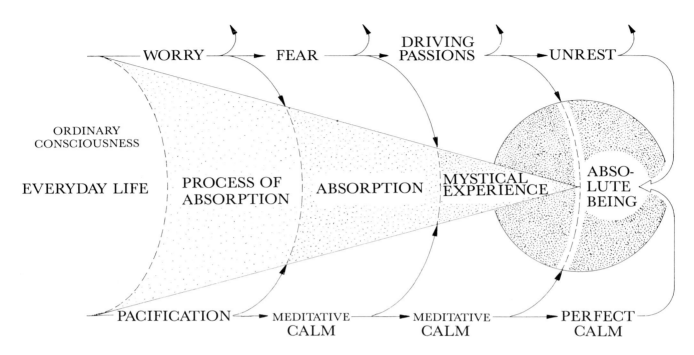

On all intuitive paths, but especially in Zen, an inner collectedness develops that leads towards absorption. Correct sitting and correct breathing contribute to this development and are capable of producing deeper levels, which can eventually lead to enlightenment. There,

however, the possibility of describing the Zen Way clearly, ends. The rest belongs to the inexpressible, to the experience which is different for everyone and for which no further images exist.

Daily Programme of a Zen *Sesshin*

In 'Shinmeikutsu' Japan*

4.00		Rise
4.20 –	5.00	*Zazen*
5.00 –	6.00	Celebration of the Eucharist
6.00 –	7.00	Breakfast and work in the house (*samu*)
7.30 –	8.10	*Zazen*
8.10 –	8.30	*Kin-hin* and a 10-minute break
8.30 –	9.40	*Teishō* and a 10-minute break
9.40 –	10.20	*Zazen* (*dokusan* 9.40–10.50)
10.20 –	10.50	*Kin-hin*
10.30 –	11.00	*Zazen*
11.00 –	11.30	Lunch
13.30 –	14.10	*Zazen*
14.10 –	14.30	*Kin-hin* and a 10-minute break
14.30 –	15.10	*Zazen* (*dokusan* 14.30–15.40)
15.10 –	15.20	Break
15.20 –	15.50	*Zazen*
15.50 –	16.30	*Zazen*
16.30 –	17.00	Supper
18.20 –	19.00	*Zazen*
19.00 –	19.20	*Kin-hin* and a 10-minute break
19.20 –	20.00	*Zazen* (*dokusan* 19.20–20.30)
20.00 –	20.20	*Kin-hin* and a 10-minute break
20.20 –	21.00	*Zazen*
21.00		Tea followed by night rest

In Europe

6.00		Rise
6.30		Tea
6.45 –	8.25	*Zazen* (3 half-hour periods)
8.30		Breakfast
9.00		Work in the house or garden (*samu*)
10.00		Coffee/Tea
10.20 –	11.20	*Teishō* (lecture by the Zen Master)
11.20 –	12.55	*Zazen* (3 half-hour periods)
11.20 –	12.50	*Dokusan*
13.00		Lunch
15.00 –	17.15	*Zazen* (4 half-hour periods)
15.30 –	16.40	*Dokusan*
17.20		Supper
18.30		Celebration of the Eucharist
19.15 –	20.50	*Zazen* (3 half-hour periods)
19.30 –	20.40	*Dokusan*
21.00		Sleep

Twice a day, in the morning and in the afternoon, there is an opportunity for *dokusan*, the personal interview with the master.

*'Shinmeikutsu' (The Cave of Divine Darkness) is Father Enomiya-Lassalle's Zen Meditation Centre in Japan. It is situated in Hinohara-Mura on the outskirts of Tokyo in a secluded nature conservation area, which is encircled on three sides by the Autumn River, a wild stream. Shinmeikutsu is the first Christian Zen meditation centre in Japan.

Glossary

Bodhidharnia: Born in Ceylon in the sixth century AD. Came to China (Canton) by sea and is considered the founder and first Patriarch of Zen in China. He practised in the mountains for nine years.

Bodhisattva: An enlightened being, who has dedicated himself to the task of helping others find liberation. In his self-mastery, wisdom and compassion he represents a high level of Buddhahood, though he is not yet a completely enlightened, perfect Buddha.

Buddha: 'The Awakened One'. Designation for the historical person Siddharta Guatama, who lived around 500 BC and later became known under the name 'Shākyamuni', i.e. 'the silent sage' (*muni*) from the clan of the Shākyas.

Buddha-nature: A concrete expression for that underlying perfect and whole nature, immanent in all creatures and things.

Dharma: The teachings of the Buddha, the universal law, the living Truth.

Dō: The Way, the highest Truth.

Dōgen: Dōgen-Zenji (1200–53), founder of Sōtō Zen. Went to China in 1223, where he studied with Master Nyojo for four years. In 1227 he returned to Japan and in 1244 founded the Eiheiji Temple. Author of the famous Zen texts 'Shōbōgenzō', 'The Treasury of the Correct Dharma Eye'.

Dōjō: The place where one practises the Way (*Zazen*).

Dokusan: (Jap.: *doku* = alone, single; *san* = going to a higher one). Private interview between master and pupil for examining correct practice.

Enlightenment: see *satori*.

Gasshō: Raising the hands with palms together as an expression of respect, gratitude, humility, or all three.

Hara: Jap. for stomach, abdomen. Hara also has a spiritual connotation as is exemplified clearly in the words of Zen Master Harada: 'You must realize that your belly is the centre of the universe.'

Harada, Daiun Sōgaku (1870–1961) was one of the most eminent Zen masters of modern Japan. Father

Enomiya-Lassalle had his first great Zen experiences with Zen Master Harada.

At the age of 7 years Daiun Sōgaku Harada became a monk in a monastery of the Sōtō School and later trained at Shōgen-ji, a monastery of the Rinzai School. At the age of 40 he became a pupil and the attendant of Dokutan Rōshi, who at that time was abbot of Nanzen-ji and the most respected Zen master of his time. After Master Dokutan awarded him the seal of transmission, 'Inka-Shōmei', he was appointed abbot of the monastery Hosshin-ji in Obama, which under his strict direction became a stronghold of genuine Zen schooling in a modern Japan no longer rich in true Zen masters. (For a more detailed account see H.M. Enomiya-Lassalle, *Zen Way to Enlightenment*.)

Hishiryo: Thinking, without thinking. Beyond thinking.

Ishin-denshin: From heart to heart, from spirit to spirit.

Jōriki: That particular strength that grows out of a collected mind (heart) as it is cultivated in Zen training through the practice of *Zazen*. Among other things, *Jōriki* enables one to be extremely alert, even in unexpected and difficult situations.

Karma: (Sanskrit; Jap. *gō*) one of the fundamental teachings of Buddhism; every action through the inevitable link of cause and effect has consequences for a future action.

Kenshō: (Jap. *ken* = to see, to behold; *shō* = nature, essence). Seeing into one's true nature. *Kenshō* and *satori* have basically the same meaning. However, it is customary to use the word '*satori*' when speaking of enlightenment, because it designates a deeper experience than the word *kenshō*.

Kin-hin: *Zazen* while walking, as it is practised between the individual sitting periods.

Kōan: originally 'law' or 'public record'. In Zen a *kōan* is a perplexing paradox that points to the ultimate Truth. *Kōans* cannot be solved through logical thinking, but only through an awakening on a deeper level of the spirit, which lies beyond discursive thinking.

Kyosaku: The wooden warning staff of the Zen master. Its use during *Zazen* has a calming as well as stimulating effect.

Makyō: (Jap. *ma* = *akuma* = devil; *kyō* = phenomena).

The appearance of 'diabolical' manifestations during the practice of *Zazen*.

Mondō: Literally: Question and answer. A Zen dialogue between master and pupil.

Mumon-kan: (Chinese, Wu-men-kuan). 'The Gateless Gate': This book with 48 *kōans* was written by Zen Master Mumon with verses and a prose commentary. Along with the 'Hegikanrōku' it is the best known *kōan* collection.

Mu: Nothing. The first and most famous *kōan* from the *Mumon-kan* is the *kōan* 'Mu'.

Rinzai: In the Zen School of the Rinzai tradition *kōans* are used in *Zazen* training and one sits facing the room.

Rōshi: (Jap. literally: a venerable, spiritual teacher or master). Traditional training in Zen takes place under the guidance of a *Rōshi*, who can also be a layman or laywoman and does not necessarily have to be a monk or a priest.

Samādhi: see *Zanmai*

Samu: Physical work. The 1–2 hours of daily work in the house or garden, which as a rule is a part of every Zen *sesshin*.

Satori: The Japanese word for the experience of enlightenment, i.e. of seeing the True Face, of opening the spiritual eye, of seeing into one's own True Nature and therefore into the True Nature of all existence.

Sesshin: *Sesshins* are days of spiritual collectedness, of intensive *Zazen* practice under the guidance of a *Rōshi*.

Shikantaza: The practice of 'just sitting'.

Shōbōgenzō: 'The Treasury of the Correct Dharma-Eye'; the principal work of Dōgen.

Sōtō: In the Sōtō School *Zazen* is practiced without a purpose or a notion of a goal and one sits facing the wall.

Tatami: A rice mat used as a ground cover for sitting.

Teishō: (Jap. *tei* = to offer, to present; *shō* = *tonaeru* = to recite, to discourse). The *Rōshi* offers *teishō* to the Buddha. It is neither an explanation, nor a commentary in the usual sense and has therefore been translated as 'exposition'.

Yamada, Kōun, born 1907, director and Zen master of the Buddhist Union 'Sanpō Kyōdan', supervisor of the foundation and direction of the San-Un-Zenhall in Kamakura, Japan, Zen master (*Rōshi*) of Father Enomiya-Lassalle, Father Willigis Jäger, Father Johannes Kopp, Pastor Gundula Meyer, Sister Annemarie Schlüter and Sister Ludwigis Fabian, among others.

Yamada Rōshi follows in the succession of Zen Master Daiun Sōgaku Harada (1870–1961) and Hakuun Ryōko Yasutani (1885–1973) (q.v.)

Yasutani, Hakuun Ryōko (1885–1973). Pupil and successor of Daiun Sōgaku Harada and until his death Zen master of Father Enomiya-Lassalle. Yasutani was one of the first genuine Zen masters to teach in the West also. In 1925 he was accepted as a pupil of Harada Rōshi and in 1943 he received the seal of transmission, 'Inka Shōmei', from him.

Like his master, Harada Rōshi, Yasutani Rōshi employed both the *shikantaza* of the Sōtō tradition as well as the use of *kōans* in his style of Zen training.

Zafu: A firm cushion filled with kapok used in the practice of *Zazen*.

Zanmai: Deep collectedness; absorption.

Zazen: Sitting in Zen, in a state of inner collectedness, in absorption.

Zen: (Chinese: *Ch'an*. Sanskrit: *dhyana*) Zen designates the process of concentration and absorption.

Zendo: The room or hall where Zen is practised.

Concise Directory of Centres Offering Zen Meditation

United Kingdom

THROSSEL HOLE PRIORY
Carrshield, Hexham, Northumberland
NE47 8AL
Main Soto Zen monastery in Britain with many affiliated
centres all over the country.

WESTERN ZEN RETREATS
Winterhead Hill Farm, Shipham, Winscombe, Avon

THE MOUSEHOLE BUDDHIST GROUP
Penaluna, Clodgy Moor, Penzance, Cornwall TR19 6UR

KANZEON — ZEN PRACTICE CENTRE TRUST
Zen Practice Centre Trust, 56 Old Orchard, Harlow, Essex
CM21 6YQ

LONDON ZEN SOCIETY
10 Belmont Street, London NW1 8HH

Five Zen Masters at the eighty-eighth birthday of Hugo M. Enomiya-Lassalle. From left to right: Father Willigis Jäger OSB, Sister Ludwigis Fabian OSB, Father Hugo M. Enomiya-Lassalle, Father Johannes Kopp SAC, Sister Annemarie Schlüter.

THE BUDDHIST SOCIETY
58 Eccleston Square, London SW1V 1PH

EDINBURGH ZEN GROUP
2 Salisbury Road, Edinburgh EH16 5AB

United States of America

SHASTA ABBEY
PO Box 199, Mt Shasta, CA 96067

MILWAUKEE ZEN CENTER
2825 N Stowell Avenue, Milwaukee, Wl 53211

THE FIRST ZEN INSTITUTE OF AMERICA
113 East 30th Street, Hinsdale, Il 60521

ZEN CENTER OF LOS ANGELES
923 South Normandie Avenue, Los Angeles, CA 90006

FURNACE MOUNTAIN ZEN CENTER
345 Jesselin Drive, Lexington, KY 40503

PROVIDENCE ZEN CENTER
528 Pound Road, Room 403, Cumberland, RI 02864

INTERNATIONAL MEDITATION CENTER USA
1331 33rd Avenue, Theravada, San Francisco, CA 94112

DAIHONZAN CHOZEN-JI INTERNATIONAL ZEN DOJO
3565 Kalihi Street, Honolulu, HI 96819

BERKELEY ZEN CENTER
1931 Russel Street, Berkeley, CA 94102

ZEN BUDDHIST TEMPLE OF CHICAGO
608 Dempster Street, Evanston, IL 60062

ZEN CENTER OF CINCINNATI
4303 Hamilton, Cincinnati, OH 45223

ALBUQUERQUE ZEN CENTER
511 Madeira SE Kogan Seiju Mammos, Albuquerque, New Mexico

Australia

BUDDHIST LODEN MAHAYANA CENTRE
175 Denison Road, Dulwich Hill, New South Wales

BUDDHIST LODEN CENTRE
10 Lomond Tee, East Brisbane, Queensland

BUDDHIST SOCIETY OF WESTERN AUSTRALIA
18 Nanson Way, Nollamara, Western Australia

BUDDHIST SOCIETY OF VICTORIA
226 Mary Street, Richmond, Victoria

BUDDHIST HOUSE CENTRE FOR ADVANCED BUDDHIST STUDIES
3 Nelson Street, Fullarton, South Australia

Sources

Frontispiece: Photograph by P. Kammann, Frankfurt. Portrait of H. M. Enomiya-Lassalle, with his Japanese and German autographs, 1986.

Page 7: Photograph by E. Stürmer, Vienna. H. M. Enomiya-Lassalle with a Japanese Zen master during a tea ceremony.

Page 8: Quotation from K. Yamada. First translated into German by Father W. Jaeger OSB.

Page 11: Photograph by P. Kammann, Frankfurt. H. M. Enomiya-Lassalle during *Zazen* with his Zen pupils at the Meditationshaus in Dietfurt/Altmühltal, Zen hall, 1986.

Page 12: Photograph by E. Stürmer, Vienna. The summons to *Zazen* in a Japanese Zen monastery.

Page 13: Quotation from Johannes Tauler, from *Der Weg der Meister*, selected texts and taken in part from old sources newly transcribed by Father Ermin Döll OFM. Published by the Meditationshaus St Franziskus, Dietfurt/Altmühltal.

Page 15: Photograph by P. Kammann, Frankfurt. H. M. Enomiya-Lassalle during a *teishō* in Dietfurt, 1986.

Page 16: Quotation from Meister Eckhart, from *Der Weg der Meister*, op. cit.
Photograph by P. Kammann, Frankfurt. Brita Dahlberg, Frankfurt, in the Full Lotus position.

Page 19: Photograph by P. Kammann, Frankfurt. H. M. Enomiya-Lassalle during a master-pupil interview, *dokusan*, 1986.

Page 20: Quotation from Zen master Hakuin, from: *Jitoku lacht den Mond an. Texte der Zen-Meister*, Vienna, 1983.

Page 22: Commentary of Zen master Mumon, cf. Zenkei Shibayama, *Zu den Quellen des Zen*, Munich, 1986, pp. 31–46.

Page 23: Photograph from the picture service of the *Süddeutsche Zeitung*, Munich. The highest mountain in Japan, Mount Fuji.

Page 25: Photograph by E. Stürmer, Vienna. H. M. Enomiya-Lassalle during *Zazen* at Shinmeikutsu near Tokyo, Zen hall, 1977.

Page 26: Photograph by E. Stürmer, Vienna. A Japanese ink drawing. Quotation from Confucius, from: *Die Weisheit des Konfuzius*, Frankfurt, 1964.

Page 27: Photograph by P. Kammann, Frankfurt. Zen hall at the Meditationshaus in Dietfurt.

Page 28: Quotation from Zen master Dōgen, from: *Jitoku lacht den Mond an*, op. cit.

Page 29: Photograph by P. Kammann, Frankfurt. Inge Ludwig from Bayreuth in the *gasshō* position, Dietfurt, 1986.

Page 31: Photograph by E. Stürmer, Vienna. *Zazen* in the garden of a Japanese Zen Monastery.

Page 32: Photograph by P. Kammann, Frankfurt. Garden by the Zen hall in Dietfurt.

Page 33: Text by Meister Eckhart, from *Der Weg der Meister*, op. cit.

Page 34: Photograph by P. Kammann, Frankfurt, H. M. Enomiya-Lassalle with Zen pupils celebrating the Eucharist in Dietfurt, 1986.

Page 36: Text by Meister Eckhart, from *Der Weg der Meister*, op. cit.

Page 37: Photograph by P. Kammann, Frankfurt. Japanese garden in the Ikebana Centre, Frankfurt.

Pages 37–8: Quotation from Ruysbroeck, from 'D. Joannis Rusbrochii Opera Omnia a.L. Surio in Latinam conversa', Coloniae, 1609.

Page 39: Photograph by P. Kammann, Frankfurt. Cloisters around the Zen hall at the Meditationshaus, Dietfurt.

Page 41: Photograph by P. Kammann, Frankfurt. Inge Ludwig from Bayreuth in walking meditation, Dietfurt, 1986.

Page 42: Quotation from Meister Eckhart, from *Der Weg der Meister*, op. cit.

Page 43: Photograph by E. Stürmer, Vienna. A special ability for concentration is necessary for Zen meditation. In Japan this is also expressed through archery. Quotation from C. Albrecht, from his *Psychologie des mystischen Bewusstseins*, Mainz, 1976.

Page 45: Photograph by J. Blätte, from his *Zazen*, © 1982 by Jakob Blätte, Waldschmidtstrasse 8a, D–8132 Tutzing. A Japanese business manager in meditative cultivation of the Zen garden in a Japanese Zen Monastery, Tokyo, 1979.

Page 46: Quotation from C. Albrecht, *Psychologie des mystischen Bewusstseins*, op. cit.

Page 47: Photograph by E. Stürmer, Vienna. A Japanese bamboo forest.

Page 48: Photograph by E. Stürmer, Vienna. The Kadō and Ikebana art developed in Japan out of Zen meditation and symbolizes the unity of heaven, earth and man.

Page 49: Quotation from Johannes Tauler, from his *Predigten*, Georg Hofmann (ed.), Freiburg 1961, and from: *Johannes Taulers Bekehrungsweg*, by Ignaz Weilner, Regensburg, 1961.
Quotation from Johannes Tauler (in box), *Der Weg der Meister*, op. cit.

Page 50: Photograph by P. Kammann, Frankfurt. The Zen hall at the Meditationshaus in Dietfurt; outside view from the garden.

Page 52: Photograph by E. Stürmer, Vienna. Stones and sand furrows in Japanese Zen gardens.

Page 55: Photograph by E. Stürmer, Vienna. *Samu*, the daily work during a Zen *sesshin*, at the Meditation Centre at Shinmeikutsu near Tokyo, 1977.
Quotation from Meister Eckhart, from *Der Weg der Meister*, op. cit.

Page 57: Photographs by E. Stürmer, Vienna. 'The Thinker' by A. Rodin as the archetype of Western rationality and 'The Awakened One' as archetype of Eastern introspection.

Page 58: Quotation from Angelus Silesius, from *Der Weg de Meister*, op. cit.

Page 59: Photograph by E. Stürmer, Vienna. The Nine-Dragon-Tree, Far Eastern symbol for timelessness.

Page 61: Photograph by R. Seitz from *Was ist der Weg—er liegt vor deinen Augen. Zen-Meditation in japanischen Gärten*, Munich, 1985.

Page 63: Quotation from Meister Eckhart, from *Der Weg der Meister*, op. cit.

Page 64: Photograph by E. Stürmer, Vienna. The Japanese Zen way: archery.

Page 67: Quotation from Angelus Silesius, from *Der Weg der Meister*, op. cit.
Quotation from Zen Master Hakuin, from *Jitoku lacht den Mond an*, op. cit.

Page 69: Photograph by R. Seitz, op. cit.

Page 71: Quotation from Angelus Silesius, from *Der Weg der Meister*, op. cit.
Photograph by E. Stürmer, Vienna. In a Japanese Zen garden.

Page 73: Photograph by R. Cieniuch, Lublin, Poland.

An ink drawing by the Korean Zen master Seung Sahn, who teaches in Poland and elsewhere (with a main seat in the USA).

Page 77: Photograph by E. Stürmer, Vienna. Japanese Zen monks.

Page 79: Photograph by R. Seitz, op. cit.

Page 80: Quotation from Zen Master Shoju Rojin, from *Jitoku lacht den Mond an*, op. cit.

Page 81: Photograph by P. Kammann, Frankfurt. Meditation lying down.

Page 82: Quotation from Zen master Dōgen, from *Jitoku lacht den Mond an*, op. cit.

Page 84: Quotations from H. M. Enomiya-Lassalle, *Zen-Meditation für Christen*, Munich, 1976; and from Zen master Dōgen, from *Jitoku lacht den Mond an*, op. cit.

Page 85: Photograph by R. Seitz, op. cit.

Page 87: Text from Angelus Silesius, from *Der Weg der Meister*, op. cit.

Page 89: Quotation from Angelus Silesius, ibid.

Page 90: Photograph by R. Seitz, op. cit.

Page 93: Photograph by E. Stürmer, Vienna. Shinmeikutsu—Cavern of Divine Darkness—The Meditation Centre of H. M. Enomiya-Lassalle, near Tokyo.

Page 94: Photograph by P. Kammann, Frankfurt. The gong to signal the beginning and the end of *Zazen* and the wooden clappers to signal the beginning and the end of *Kin-hin*, meditative walking.
Quotation from Meister Eckhart, from *Der Weg der Meister*, op. cit.
Quotation from Zen master Dōgen, from *Jitoku lacht den Mond an*, op. cit.

Pages 95–9: The collection of exercises was inspired by, among others: *Jane Fonda's Workout Book*, Penguin, 1984; M. Gach, *Aku-yoga, Gesund durch Fluss der Lebenskräfte. Ein praktisches Übungsbuch*, Munich, 1985. Photographs by P. Kammann, Frankfurt. Demonstration of the exercises by Susanne Hagenstein, Mühlheim, and Andreas Heyden, Frankfurt.

Pages 100–3: Photographs by P. Kammann, Frankfurt. Demonstration of the exercises by Brita Dahlberg, Andreas Heyden, Inge Ludwig and Susanne Hagenstein.

Pages 104–6: Photographs by P. Kammann, Frankfurt.

Demonstration of the exercises by Brita Dahlberg and Andreas Heyden.

Page 106: Positions for *kin-hin*, according to K. Graf Dürkheim, *Übung des Leibes*, Munich, 1981, p. 80f.

Page 107: Photograph by P. Kammann, Frankfurt. H. M. Enomiya-Lassalle in meditative walking, *kin-hin*, with his pupils at a Zen *sesshin* in the Zen hall in Dietfurt.

Page 108: Illustrations from H. Lodes, *Atme richtig. Der Schlüssel zu Gesundheit und Ausgeglichenheit*, Munich, 1977, p. 24.

Page 110: Illustrations from *Religion am Gymnasium, 11*, compiled by Walter Lang, Munich, 1982, p. 195.

Page 111: Illustration and description according to W. Massa (ed.), *Kontemplative Meditation*, Mainz, second edition, 1975, p. 10f.

Page 112: Illustration from *Religion am Gymnasium, 11*, op. cit. p. 160

Pages 114–15: Glossary according to *Lexikon der östlichen Weisheitslehren*, Munich, 1986.

Page 116: Photograph by P. Kammann, Frankfurt. Dietfurt, 1986.

Index

THE HEART OF BUDDHISM

GUY CLAXTON

At the heart of Buddhism is a Buddhism of the heart. The religion for a secular age, it offers a practical, comprehensible way to achieve more peace of mind and generosity of spirit. Concerning itself primarily with improving the quality of everyday life, it requires no adherence to obscure or magical beliefs, and offers a penetrating diagnosis of the human condition as well as a powerful and proven set of techniques for overcoming the rigours of today's world, both at home and at work.

This easy-to-read book gives an insight into the essence of Buddhism. Guy Claxton explains why Buddhism is so appropriate to our individual, social and global predicament and goes on to describe how we can help ourselves individually, with a teacher, or in a group, through understanding, meditation, communication and discipline.

An excellent introduction for newcomers to Buddhism as well as a useful reference for Buddhist students, *The Heart of Buddhism* relates the main tenets of Buddhism clearly to the quality of ordinary modern daily life.

THE ESSENCE OF SPIRITUAL PHILOSOPHY

HARIDAS CHAUDHURI

This book brings together selections from the writings and lectures of the distinguished spiritual teacher Haridas Chaudhuri. Weaving together Eastern and Western thought, Dr Chaudhuri, using his own special philosophical perspective, shows how an evolution of consciousness is taking place on both individual and collective levels towards a state of awareness which truly integrates spirit within matter on all levels of existence.

Human beings are by nature spiritual, and the fulfillment of our spiritual potential should be the principal work in the life of each person so that wholeness, balance, harmony and integration can help us toward the creation of the kingdom of heaven on earth. Dr Chaudhuri's teachings provide valuable guidance as to how this fulfillment may be achieved, ranging over such diverse subjects as the problems of faith, free will and determinism, and the nature and practice of meditation. His work also includes modern theories of depth psychology as well as ancient mystical traditions.

The challenge of this book — as of the era to come — is to be aware of, assimilate, respond to and assist in creating this potential dynamic age of synthesis, allowing the deepest dreams of mankind to come true.

YOGA: THE TECHNOLOGY OF ECSTASY

GEORG FEUERSTEIN

The impulse towards transcendence is intrinsic to human life. Nowhere has this drive found a more consistent and versatile expression than in India, whose civilization has spawned an overwhelming variety of spiritual beliefs, practices and approaches. The goal of Yoga, the most famous and globally widespread of India's spiritual traditions, is to take us beyond ourselves to the Absolute Reality, to the utterly blissful union of the individual self with the transcendental Divine.

In recent decades Yoga, once known only in the East, has spread across the world to become a household word. In spite of the wealth of books published on the subject, the historical origins and philosophical underpinnings of this rich and varied spiritual technology have remained obscure even to its millions of Western practitioners. *Yoga: The Technology of Ecstasy* is a work of unparalleled scope that at last weaves the daunting complexity of five thousand years of Yoga into a single tapestry, outlining its relationship with other important Indian traditions and discussing the diverse forms it has taken in Hinduism, Buddhism and Jainism. Here too is a clear, comprehensive and systematic overview of the history, philosophy and practice of every major branch of Yoga, including Hatha-Yoga and Tantra, which have gained wide followings in the West.

Speaking always to the contemporary reader, Georg Feuerstein offers a compelling and relevant articulation of Yoga's profound life-transforming value for modern men and women.

THE WAY OF NON-ATTACHMENT

DHIRAVAMSA

The most important goal in meditation is
freedom, and this can be achieved through
gradual release from the grip of ideas. In this
practical handbook of Vipassana meditation
the author describes a simple but powerful
technique for gaining true freedom — peace,
happiness, and understanding.

The key to this revolution within the mind
is the conquest of desire. Desire causes much
pain and distress, and to end it we must
transcend it and view things objectively.
Freedom from desire will bring alertness,
clarity of mind, and insight, and through
Insight Meditation you will gradually become
aware of the light of truth.

*Born in Thailand and trained as a monk, Dhiravamsa
is one of the most creative representatives of Theravada
Buddhism in the West. He is solidly grounded in his
oriental apprenticeship of meditation and abhidharma
and has evolved an easy improvisational style of teaching.*